The Young Vic Theatre Company presents

Peribanez

by Lope de Vega

English version by Tanya Ronder

First performance 1 May 2003
Young Vic 66 The Cut, London SE1

www.youngvic.org

THE YOUNG VIC (A REGISTERED CHARITY 268876) RECEIVES PUBLIC FUNDING FROM:

Young Vic

Lambeth Arts

Association of
London Government

Southwark.
Council

ARTS COUNCIL
ENGLAND

Peribanez

Cast

Peribanez	**Michael Nardone**
Casilda	**Jackie Morrison**
Commander	**David Harewood**
Ines	**Mali Harries**
Leonardo	**Mark Lockyer**
Lujan	**Paul Hamilton**
Costanza/Queen	**Rhiannon Meades**
Anton/Constable	**Jason Baughan**
Benito/Arceo	**Robert Willox**
Priest/Painter/Helipe/Lisardo	**Michael O'Connor**
King/Mendo/Valerio	**Gregory Fox-Murphy**
Llorente/Florez	**Vincent Patrick**
Gil and Master Musician	**John A Sampson**

Running time 2 hours 30 minutes including interval.

Please turn off mobile phones, pagers and watch alarms.

PRODUCTION CREDITS

Electrician	Graham Parker
Costumes	Angels, London New York wigs
	Cheryl Glover
Set	The Blue Reef Projects Ltd,
	Young Vic Worksop
Crew	Adriano Austino, Pete Elvin,
	Dave Kerry, Sean Mooney,
	Simon Plumridge, Neil Sutcliffe,
	Simon Tachev, John Tibbort

With thanks to John Kenton, RNT Music Department, Dave Adcock, Musical Instrument Repairs & Sales, Carol Ayles, ADM Milling Ltd, Alan, Andy's Guitar Centre and Workshop, Terry Goulden, Arms and Archery, Almeida Theatre, Lino-De-Bruyn, Mick Etherington, News International Newspapers Ltd, Carol Grimes

Wardrobe care provided by Lever Brothers

Young Vic

Direction	**Rufus Norris**
Design	**Ian MacNeil**
Costumes	**Tania Spooner**
Lighting	**Rick Fisher**
Sound	**Paul Arditti**
Music	**Orlando Gough**
Choreography	**Scarlett Mackmin**
Musical Direction	**Jonathan Gill**
Casting	**Wendy Spon**
Fight Direction	**Terry King**
Assistant Director and Master of Horse	**Nizar Zuabi**
Design Production Assistant	**Anna Bruder**
Design Studio Assistants	**Jamie Todd**
	Adam Wiltshire
Costume Supervision	**Sarah Bowern**
Stage Manager	**Charlotte Geeves**
Deputy Stage Manager	**Clare Loxley**
Assistant Stage Manager	**Dean Rees**
Lighting Board Programmer	**Rachel Bowen**
Sound Operator	**Sarah Weltman**
Dresser	**Jo Tucker**
Research	**Thea Jones**
Literal Translation	**Simon Scardifield**

Peribanez

The Company

JASON BAUGHAN Theatre includes: *The Three Sisters; Have You Anything To Declare; Caucasian Chalk Circle* (Orange Tree Theatre); *Clockwatching; Whispers Along The Patio* (Orange Tree/ Stephen Joseph Theatre); *Twelfth Night; The Tempest; Measure For Measure* (RSC); *The Dove* (Croyden Warehouse); *Tales From The Magic Storybowl* (Bolton Octagon); *A Midsummer Night's Dream* (Mappa Mundi); *Much Ado About Nothing* (Actors from the London Stage). TV includes: *Doctors* (BBC); *The Bill* (Thames).

GREGORY FOX-MURPHY Theatre includes: *Kafka's Dick* (Salisbury Playhouse); *The Taming of the Shrew* (Tokyo Globe); *Journey's End* (Courtyard Theatre); *Observe the Sons of Ulster Marching Towards the Somme* (The Caird Company); *As You Like It; Twelfth Night* (Natural Perspectives Theatre Company); *The Woman Who Thought She Was A Dog* (Fringe First Winner; Edinburgh Festival); *Ghetto* (Oxford Playhouse); *A Christmas Carol* (Vanessa Ford Productions). TV includes: *The Key; Murder Rooms: The Dark Beginnings of Sherlock Holmes; Casualty* (BBC).

PAUL HAMILTON Theatre includes: *Troilus and Cressida; Everyman; The Mysteries* (RSC); *Out Of A House…* (National Theatre); *The Crucible; Frankenstein* (Leicester Haymarket); *A Streetcar Named Desire* (Royal Lyceum; Edinburgh); *The Three Lives of Lucie Cabrol* (Theatre de Complicite); *Gormenghast* (David Glass); *Of Mice and Men* (Harrogate Theatre Royal); *La Bete Humaine* (Nottingham Playhouse).TV includes: *Henry VI Parts 1 and 2* (BBC/RSC) and *Badger*. Film includes: *Bridget Jones's Diary* and *The Gathering* (Granada/Samuelson).

DAVID HAREWOOD Theatre includes: Othello in *Othello* (National Theatre); Alceste in *The Misanthrope* (Chichester Minerva); Romeo in *Romeo and Juliet* (National Theatre tour) Sloane in *Entertaining Mr Sloane* (Derby Playhouse); Edmund in *King Lear* (Talawa Theatre); Antony in *Antony and Cleopatra* (New York Public Theatre); *The Rivals* (West Yorkshire Playhouse); *Black Poppies* (Theatre Royal Stratford East/BBC). TV includes: *The Vice* (Carlton); *Babyfather; Murder Most Horrid* (BBC); *A&E* (ITV); *Harry Enfield and Chums* (Tiger Aspect); *Hearts and Minds* (Channel 4); *Bermuda Grace* (ITV/NBC co-production).

MALI HARRIES Theatre includes: *La Lupa; The Rivals; Henry IV Part 1* (RSC); *A Christmas Carol* (Chichester Theatre); *Four Nights in Knaresborough* (Tricycle, Kilburn); *Our Country's Good* (Out of Joint); *Romeo and Juliet* (The Swan, Worcester). Radio includes: *Dionysos; Blind; Pembroke Arcadia; Tales of Murasaki* (BBC Radio 4). TV includes: *Byron; Inspector Lynley Mysteries; Final Demand; Dalziel and Pascoe* (BBC); *Foyles War* (ITV); *Not Getting Any* (BBC 2W).

MARK LOCKYER Theatre includes: *Outbreak Of God in Area 9* (Young Vic); *The Ragged Trousered Philanthropists* (Theatre Royal Stratford East); *Ghetto; Fuenteovejuna; The Madness of George III* (National Theatre); *The Clink* (Riverside Studios); *The Prisoner of Zenda* (Greenwich Theatre); *King Lear; The Merchant of Venice; The Tempest; Romeo and Juliet; The Taming Of The Shrew* (RSC); *The Cherry Orchard* (RSC/West End); *Hamlet* (The Globe Theatre); *Ion* (The Gate Theatre).

Young Vic

RHIANNON MEADES Theatre includes: *The Vagina Monologues* (The Gate Theatre); *The View From The Porch* (The King's Head Theatre); *The Elixir of Love* (ENO); *Never Never Land* (BAC); *The Woman Who Swallowed A Pin* (The Lab at Southwark Playhouse); The Provoked Wife (Mercury Theatre, Colchester); *The Threepenny Opera* (Pimlico Opera); *Prospero's Children* (Quicksilver Theatre); *Heartbreak House* (Shaw's Corner); *Annajanska; The Man of Destiny* (International Theatre, Rome); *Lady From The Sea* (The Bridewell Theatre).TV includes: *The Bill* (ITV).

JACKIE MORRISON Theatre includes: *Sadly Solo Joe* (Greenwich Theatre); *Oh What A Lovely War* (National Theatre tour and Roundhouse); *Celaine* (Hampstead Theatre); *Othello* (Watermill Theatre); *The Prime of Miss Jean Brodie* (Strand); *When We Are Married* (Savoy); *What Every Woman Knows; Candida* (Stephen Joseph Theatre); *A Midsummer Night's Dream* (ESC). TV includes: *Ultimate Force* (2 series, ITV); *Casualty* (BBC); *Taggart; Dr Finlay* (2 Series, STV) *Head over Heels* (Carlton); *Underbelly* (BBC).

MICHAEL NARDONE Theatre includes: *Gargarin Way* (National Theatre/Traverse); *Victoria* (RSC); *Knives in Hens* (Traverse/Bush); *Speculator* (Traverse/Edinburgh Festival); *Marriage of Figaro* (Royal Lyceum, Edinburgh); *Cyrano De Bergerac* (Communicado/Almeida); *The Collection* (Traverse); *Merlin 1&2* (Royal Lyceum); *The Satyre of the Fourth Estate* (Wildcat/Edinburgh Festival). TV includes: *Rose and Maloney* (ITV); *Looking After Jo-Jo; Silent Witness* (BBC); *Ultimate Force; Wycliffe; Inspector Rebus* (ITV).

MICHAEL O'CONNOR Theatre includes: *Ghetto; Sunday in the Park With George; The Shaughraun; Piano* (National Theatre); *The Tempest* (RSC); *The Terrible Voice of Satan; The Knocky* (Royal Court); *Twelfth Night* (Manchester Royal Exchange); *The Marriage of Figaro* (Sheffield Crucible); *Bombing People* (Jermyn Street Theatre); *Outskirts* (Birmingham Rep); *Sweeney Todd* (New Vic, Stoke). TV includes: *Hardware* (LWT); *The Bill* (Thames); *Asylum* (Paramount).

VINCENT PATRICK Theatre includes: *Stones in His Pockets* (Duke of York's Theatre); *The Beauty Queen of Leenane* (New Vic, Stoke); *A Skull in Connemara* (Bolton Octagon); *Crying in the Chapel* (Yard Theatre), *3am* and *Faces for Places* (Trinity Players). Radio includes: *The Furys; The Growing Summer; Shirley* (BBC Radio 4). TV includes: *Do You Remember* (BBC). Film includes: *Bolt* (RTE); *The Amp* (UCD Productions); *Salome* (Pinback Productions).

JOHN A SAMPSON Theatre includes: *Scarlatti's Birthday Party* (Natural Theatre Company); *Fiddler on the Roof* (Courtyard, Hereford); *Macbeth* (Demarco/Edinburgh Festival); *The Satyre of the Fourth Estate* (John Maygrath, Edinburgh Festival); *Good* (Tron/Edinburgh Festival); *Volpone* (Edinburgh Lyceum); *Hecuba* (Winged Horse Theatre Company) *Beggars Opera* (Pename Theatre Co); *Desire* (Communicado Theatre); *The Feast of the Pheasant* (Scottish Early Music Consort); *Border Warfare; John Brown's Body* (Wildcat/Channel 4); *The Big Picnic* (Bill Brydon Productions/BBC2). TV includes: *Rab C Nesbit* (BBC); *The Baldy Man* (Carlton).

ROBERT WILLOX Theatre includes: *Rutherford & Son* (Salisbury Playhouse); *The Colour of Justice* (Tricycle Theatre); *Troilus & Cressida; A Month in the Country* (RSC); *The Snow Palace* (Sphinx Theatre); *King Lear; The Visit* (Sydney Theatre Company); *Antony and Cleopatra* (Australian People's Theatre). TV includes: *Spooks; 2000 Acres of Skye; Monarch of the Glen* (BBC); *Ultimate Force* (ITV). Film includes: *League of Extraordinary Gentlemen* (20th Century Fox); *Den of Lions* (US); *Julius Caesar* (Italy).

Peribanez

RUFUS NORRIS – DIRECTION Theatre includes: *Sleeping Beauty* & *Afore Night Come* (Young Vic) for which he won the Evening Standard Award 2001 for Outstanding Newcomer; *Dirty Butterfly* (Soho Theatre); *Tall Stories* (BAC/Vienna Festival); *Small Change* (Sheffield Crucible); *Mish A Ruman* (Al Kasaba, Ramallah); *Under The Blue Sky* & *About The Boy* (Royal Court); *My Dad's Cornershop* (Birmingham Rep); *Strike Gently*; *The Art Of Random Whistling* & *The People Downstairs* (Young Vic Studio/Wink); *The Lizzie Play*; *Rosa Carnivora* & *Waking Beauty* (Arts Threshold/Wink). Rufus was awarded an Arts Foundation Fellowship in 2002 and is an Associate Director of the Young Vic.

TANYA RONDER – ADAPTION Tanya trained at Rada and has worked as an actress for the last fourteen years, mostly in classical theatre. She has played at the Royal Exchange, the National Theatre, West Yorkshire Playhouse, the Royal Court, the Young Vic, Theatre Royal Bath, the Gate Theatre, Oxford Playhouse, Salisbury Playhouse, Traverse Theatre, Theatre Clywd and others. She has been quietly writing for years. This is her first adaptation.

IAN MACNEIL – DESIGN Theatre includes: *Afore Night Come* (Young Vic); *Far Away* (also New York Theatre Workshop); *Via Dolorosa* (also Broadway & Duchess Theatre; West End); *This Is A Chair*; *Body Talk*; *The Editing Process*; *Death And The Maiden* (also National Tour); *Plasticine* & *A Number* (all Royal Court); *Albert Speer*; *Machinal*; *An Inspector Calls* (National Theatre); *The Ingolstadt Plays*; *Figaro Gets Divorced*; *Jerker* (Gate Theatre); *The Picture of Dorian Gray* (Lyric, Hammersmith); *Enter Achilles*; *Bound to Please* (DV8). TV includes: *Winterreise* (Channel 4). Film includes: *Eight* (Working Title); *The Hours* (Paramount – as Associate Producer). Awards include: Olivier Award for Best Opera (*Tristan and Isolde*); Critics Circle Award

(*Machinal* & *An Inspector Calls*); Olivier Award for Design (*An Inspector Calls*); Tony Nomination for Best Design (*An Inspector Calls*, Broadway); 2002 Evening Standard Award for Best Designer (*Plasticine* & *A Number*).

TANIA SPOONER – COSTUMES Previous theatre credits include: *The Rake's Progress* (Hannover Opera); *Mare Nostrum* (Theatre Basel); *Kantan* & *Damask Drum* (Almeida Opera); *Eugene Onegin* (Theatre Basal); *The Pleasure Man* (Citizen's Theatre); *Cosi Fan Tutte* (Opera North); *Guys and Dolls* (Pimlico Opera); *West Side Story* (Pimlico Opera); *The Widowing of Mrs Holroyd*; *A Collier's Friday Night*; *Machinal* (Battersea Arts Centre); *The Boy Who Left Home* (Riverside Studios); *Shipyard Tales* (Welfare State International); *Eugene Onegin* (Oxford Playhouse); *Magic Mirrors* (Leicester Haymarket); *The Kitchen of Life* (BAC).

RICK FISHER – LIGHTING Theatre includes: *Red Demon*, *Afore Night Come* (Young Vic); *Jerry Springer the Opera* (National Theatre & Edinburgh Festival); *Far Away* (New York); *A Number* (Royal Court); *Lobby Heroes* (Donmar); *A Russian In The Woods* (RSC); *Mother Clap's Molly House* (National Theatre); *A Boston Marriage* (Donmar); *Blue/Orange* (National Theatre & West End); Disney's *The Hunchback of Notre Dame* (Berlin); *Via Dolorosa* (Royal Court & Broadway). Olivier Award winner for Best Lighting Design include *Lady in the Dark*, *Chips with Everything*, *Machinal* (all at National Theatre).

PAUL ARDITTI – SOUND Theatre includes: *Sleeping Beauty*, *Afore Night Come*; *Homebody/ Kabul* (Young Vic); *Three Sisters* (West End); *Dirty Butterfly* (Soho); *Accidental Death of an Anarchist* (Donmar); *My Brilliant Divorce* (West End); *Auntie and Me* (West End); *Twelfth Night* & *Uncle Vanya* (Donmar, New York); *Far Away* (New York, Lucille Lortel 2003 sound design award nomination). As resident Sound Designer at the Royal Court

1993-2002, over 70 shows including *Plasticine; Boy Gets Girl; Mouth to Mouth; Blasted; The Kitchen; Some Voices; Mojo; The Weir; Via Dolorosa; Attempts On Her Life; My Night With Reg; Hysteria; This is A Chair*. Other theatre: *The Steward of Christendom, Blue Heart, Hinterland* (Out Of Joint); *The Beauty Queen of Leenane* (Druid); *The Chairs* (Complicite, Drama Desk nomination in New York); *Romeo and Juliet* (Chichester); *Tales From Hollywood* (Donmar); *Light* (Complicite); *The Lonesome West* (Broadway); *Hamlet, The Tempest* (RSC); *Orpheus Descending* (West End & Broadway); *Doctor Doolittle* (West End). Awards include: Drama Desk Award for Outstanding Sound Design in 1992 for the music theatre piece *Four Baboons Adoring The Sun* (Broadway).

ORLANDO GOUGH – MUSIC Recent work includes: *This House Will Burn*, choreographed by Ashley Page for the Royal Ballet, *Of Oil & Water*, a dance piece choreographed by Siobhan Davies, music for *The Tempest* (RSC), & *Birds On Fire* for the viol consort Fretwork. With the composer & singer Richard Crew, Orlando started the sixteen-piece choir *The Shout*, which last year toured its music-theatre piece *Tall Stories* to venues in England, Europe & America. Together, Richard & Orlando have written four large choral pieces: *The Shouting Fence* (South Bank Centre 1998), *Corona*, first performed in Cornwall on occasion of the total solar eclipse in 1999, *Journey To The North* for children (2000), & *Sea Tongue*, premiered at Huddersfield Contemporary Music Festival, November 2001. *Because I Sing*, for 16 amateur choirs & *The Shout*, directed by Alain Platel, was performed at the Roundhouse in March 2001. Orlando was a founder member of the bands *The Lost Jockey* & *Man Jumping*. He won the Time Out Classical Musician of the Year 2002. Future projects include commissions for the Crouch End Festival Chorus, Scottish Ballet & ENO.

SCARLETT MACKMIN – CHOREOGRAPHY Theatre includes: *Sleeping Beauty* (Young Vic); *The Merry Wives of Windsor* (RSC/Michigan/Tour); *The Tempest* (Sheffield Crucible/Old Vic); *The Arbor* & *Iphigenia* (Sheffield Crucible); *Up on the Roof* (Chichester); *Privates on Parade* (Donmar, Oliver Award Nomination); *In Flame* (New Ambassadors & Bush); *Air Swimming* (BAC & tour); *Luminous* (Butler's Wharf); *Tabula rasa* (Flynn, USA). Film includes: *Chocolat* (Miramax); *The Last Minute* (Palm Pictures); *Miss Julie* (Mike Figgis/Red Mullet).

JONATHAN GILL – MUSICAL DIRECTION Theatre includes: *Sleeping Beauty* (Young Vic); *The Marriage of Figaro* (New Vic Stoke/Stephen Joseph, Scarborough); *The Car Man* (Old Vic); *Oklahoma!* (National Theatre); *Of Thee I Sing* (Bridewell); *Company* (Library Theatre Manchester); *The Good Companions* (Keswick Theatre By The Lake); *Singin' In The Rain* (West Yorkshire Playhouse) & *The Dreaming* (Linbury Theatre, Royal Opera House). Opera includes: *Cavalleria Russicana* & *Pugliucci* (Opera Holland Park); *Macbeth* (ETO); *La Boheme* & *Cosi Fan Tutte* (Drill Hall & Stadsschouwberg, Amsterdam), *On Thee We Feed* & *Shawna and Ron's Half Moon* (Bayliss Programme at ENO) & *The Hackney Chronicles* (Hackney Music Development Trust).

NIZAR ZUABI – ASSISTANT DIRECTOR AND MASTER OF HORSE Nizar graduated from the Nesan Nativ Acting Studio, Jerusalem in 1997. As a director his theatre credits include: *Long Way, Friends* & *Alive From Palestine* (World Tour, including Young Vic) all for Al Kasaba Theatre. As an actor his theatre includes: *Spring Awakening* & *Chekov Stories* (Tsavta Theatre, Tel-Aviv), *Zir Sallem* & *Mish A Ruman* (Al Kassaba Theatre). Film credits include: Lover (Roberto Fanza) and The Battle on Tel May (Oded Raskin).

Peribanez

The Young Vic Theatre Company

The Young Vic is a theatre for everyone - but especially the young.

We present seasons of classic plays - old and new (and each year we create a theatrical event that embraces young people, children and adults in a single experience).

At the heart of our work is our auditorium. Its unique, humane proportions express and influence everything we as a company feel and think and do. Built out of humdrum materials - breezeblock and steel - it's a machine for the imagination, generating fantasy and debate with equal enthusiasm. No one sits more than six rows from the stage. The seats are unreserved yet each has a perfect view. It's big enough to house a whole society but small enough to be filled by a single gesture. It's a theatre for a democracy - a people's theatre for an engaged, imaginative audience.

Through accidents or history, many people, especially the young, believe that theatre belongs to 'other people' of another class or another generation. But artists create for the whole world. So for each of our main house shows we prepare an extensive programme of Teaching, Participation and Research aimed at our local schools and colleges. We offer on-stage workshops, an annual Schools' Theatre Festival and packs of resource material for every production. We provide an extensive work-experience and apprenticeship programme for young people. All this is offered free of charge. Each year thousands of young people from our local boroughs of Lambeth and Southwark benefit from these schemes. One of our core ideas is that by teaching others about theatre we learn.

Our aim is to be this country's leading home for younger theatre artists, especially directors. In 2001 we began to present seasons of work by new directors in tandem with productions by some of the great directors of the world. By mingling youth and experience, ambition and genius we hope to make the Young Vic one of the most exciting theatres in the world.

Around 100,000 people visit us in London each year and thousands more on tour. We keep our prices as low as we can and make a priority of finding new audiences. Our Funded Ticket Scheme offers free tickets to all school age children in Lambeth and Southwark and our innovative 'Two Boroughs Project', launched in 2001, offers every local resident of Lambeth and Southwark the chance to visit one of our productions for nothing.

We receive public funding from Arts Council England, the Association of London Government and Lambeth and Southwark Councils. This makes up a third of our income. A further third is generated through box office and touring. The remaining third has to be found by our Development Department from sponsorship and gifts from supporters.

We believe a theatre should be a place of energy, intelligence and pleasure. Join us whenever you can.

Young Vic

Supporting the Young Vic

Since its earliest days, the Young Vic has counted on the support of many enlightened partners. Their commitment to our work has enabled us to establish an international reputation for presenting great plays - classics and new work - in exciting, innovative productions.

TO BUILD ON THIS SUCCESS WE NEED YOUR HELP

We are grateful to our public funders - Arts Council England, The Association of London Government and Lambeth and Southwark Councils - for their contribution to our work. But, public funding and the box office provide only two thirds of our income. The remainder, some £1 million a year, must be raised through sponsorship, trust donations and private contributors so we can mount our productions, give opportunities to young artists and do our ground-breaking work in schools and with the local community.

By joining the Supporters' Scheme you make our work possible. For example:

FRIENDS (£30)
buys the materials for the design team to make one stage prop

BACKSTAGE CREW (£100)
enables twenty-five local young people to go to the theatre for the first time for free as part of our Funded Ticket Scheme

SUPPORTING CAST (£350)
pays for one On Stage Schools Workshop

LEADING ROLE (£600)
pays for one week's hire of a rehearsal room

STAGE PARTNER (£1000)
pays for a Young Director to work with actors in our studio for a week

Every donation is vital, helping ensure our future. Please join us as a Supporter. Or, if you are able, make a greater contribution through The Director's Circle. To find out more pick up a leaflet in the foyer or call the Development Office on 020 7922 8400.

BE PART OF OUR FUTURE

Peribanez

The Young Vic Supporters

Young Vic

Young Vic

The Young Vic Company

PERIBANEZ

Lope de Vega

English version by Tanya Ronder

To David

with thanks

Lope de Vega and 'Peribanez y el Comendador de Ocana'

Lope de Vega (1562–1635) was reading Spanish and Latin and composing verses before he was five. Meanwhile Shakespeare, age three and a half, was cutting his teeth in the English countryside.

Lope's life was full – so full it's hard to imagine how he fitted it all in. As an adult he was a poet, a sailor on the Spanish Armarda (using poems to a faithless lover to clean his gun), an Inquisitor, had long-lasting affairs with two actresses, married twice and became a father at least six times. He was secretary to two Dukes, killed a man, served a prison sentence, lived in the country and in the town, was an avid gardener and was exiled from Madrid for fouling his ex-lover's name. He became a priest and then lived bigamously with two women in two homes, was widowed, brought up a household of four children from different mothers on his own – and wrote plays. As many, it's believed, as eight hundred. Only half survive but the ones we have are as varied and full of life as his years on earth.

Lope wrote at a time of change for Spain, when towns were growing into cities. As a result of high taxes and political unrest, the population could no longer rely on the earth for their livelihood. Peasant life on the land was dwindling. Lope wasn't the first playwright to idealise this rural life – which belonged to his grandparents' generation – but he was one of the few to have sampled it first-hand. His peasant world, from which so many of his plays derive, is beautifully detailed. It's an earthy world peopled with animals and characterised by a lack of guile. He places the peasant at the centre of this work politically – and emotionally too. Their inner lives and spoken word are more full of poetry, passion, intelligence and self-knowledge than his (often ridiculed) high-born Nobles, Commanders and Royals.

The landless, rural poor were his main interest and, largely, his audience. At the time of writing *Peribanez y el Comendador de*

Ocana, somewhere between 1605 and 1614, there was no way a peasant farmer such as Peribanez could have had access to the King. He didn't – possibly couldn't – flout all that his society held dear and break such rules, so he has the Commander knight Peribanez during the course of the action and bypasses this difficulty, allowing Peribanez and the king to meet face to face and for the King to save our hero's life.

First and foremost Lope de Vega was a people's playwright. He wrote to entertain. The darker strands in his work nearly always gave way to a happy outcome, even after a costly, bloody journey. He was master of the tragi-comedy. And he vigorously upheld the belief that this was a playwright's job – to entertain the masses . . . 'Give pleasure to the people and let art be hanged.'

In his ironic treatise about the new art of writing plays (*El Arte nuevo de hacer comedias en este tiempo,* published 1609), he divided his audience into those who favoured either this 'new art' championed and created by himself, or the stiffer, literary plays of the older generation. The speed at which he wrote (he complained he spent his life sharpening quills) produced a huge range of plays without concern for consistency of subject or form. For inspiration he drew on chronicles and legends, history and myths, oriental and Italian stories, sacred and chivalrous tomes and popular songs. He did, however, develop highly sophisticated verse forms where the verbal structure helped his audience grasp what was happening. They grew to expect the witty 'gracioso' from the metre in the first line of his speech.

Lope filled Madrid's two theatres, the Corral de la Cruz and Corral del Principe, year after year with rowdy and insatiable audiences. They were daytime shows, presented on a plain apron stage with audience (male) in tiers of seats on three sides, no scenery – only a curtain along the back through which actors could enter. Above the stage, held up on pillars, was a gallery for musicians where certain scenes took place. There were 'groundlings' (again, men only) who stood at the front and women crowded together in an enclosure at the back. The rich, male and female, watched from boxes which were the windows of houses surrounding the open courtyard.

Plays rarely ran for more than a week. Reviews were spontaneous in the shape of orange peel and soft fruit ('Get off!') or rattles and whistles ('More please'). Lope introduced onto these stages integral music, horses, dancing and other fusions of life. The sixty years during which his plays were performed (he started at twelve and wrote tirelessly, an average of twenty pages a day; his contemporary biographer, Montalvan, asserting that Lope could write a play after mass while his breakfast was warming) forms, along with the plays of Cervantes and Calderon, the Spanish Golden Age.

Although bent on entertainment, the humanist in Lope couldn't help but spill over every page of his work. He knew and loved people; he also knew pain, grief, torture, suffering. His worlds are full of disappointment, temptation and loss in the midst of extreme joy and irrepressible humour. A bonus for us is that his women are as rounded as his men. They are strong, full-blooded, hot-tempered and canny. They may be honest and pure-hearted but they are fallible too. Lope's complex life of intimacy with women is thrown straight back onto the stage, breeding vivid and believable creatures, often embodying a force both natural and vital. Likewise his notion of honour. He doesn't challenge the beliefs of the day but for Lope 'honour' is more ample and human than the received notion, the prerogative of Noblemen. He invests all his characters with self-respect. The central plot of *Peribanez* unfurls as a result of a peasant's sense of his offended honour.

Lope's death prompted a state funeral that lasted nine days – long enough, I guess, for people to mourn the loss of all those different lives lived by one extremely brilliant and passionate man. 'Es de Lope' – 'it's real Lope' – has entered the Spanish language as shorthand for anything of excellence.

Tanya Ronder

Characters

PERIBANEZ, *farmer, Casilda's husband*
CASILDA, *Peribanez' wife*

INES, *cousin and best friend to Casilda*
COSTANZA, *cousin and friend to Casilda*

THE PRIEST, *uncle to Casilda*

COMMANDER *of Ocana*
LUJAN, *looks after Commander's animals*
LEONARDO, *Commander's right-hand man*
FLOREZ, *young servant to Commander*

KING *Enrique the third*
QUEEN, *his wife*
ARCEO, *secretary to the King*

CONSTABLE, *the state officer of the highest rank for Toledo*
PAINTER, *from Toledo*

ANTON, *friend and neighbour to Peribanez*
BENITO, *older village man and harvester*
GIL, *village man and local musician*

MENDO, *harvester*
HELIPE, *harvester*
LLORENTE, *harvester and singer*
CHAPARRO, *harvester*

LISARDO, *musician*
VALERIO, *musician*

ACT ONE

Scene One

PERIBANEZ' *house. A small wedding party arrives accompanied by the end of some music played by* GIL *and other* GUESTS *who have played on their walk from Church.*

INES (*to the newly-married* CASILDA). You're married!

CASILDA. I'm married!

COSTANZA (*to* CASILDA). Mrs Ibanez.

INES. What can I wish you? I wish you the best of everything, hundreds of children and endless years of happiness together.

COSTANZA. 'Til you're almost immortal!

CASILDA. Years full of friendship with you my cousins.

THE PRIEST. I don't want to throw water on the fire, I'm sure you don't mean to insult God but it's unnecessary, this over baking the pudding. Nothing means more than the marriage ceremony, no amount of compliments – I've said words enough – there's nothing more to be said, by family or friend. Or Priest.

INES. We're just adding 'good luck' Father . . . 'though of course you know best.

THE PRIEST. Send your wishes up to Heaven! He's the one who'll answer your prayers. He rewards the virtuous and my niece is a good, sensible girl.

ANTON. Ah but will she be a jealous wife?

CASILDA. Ah but will she need to be?

INES. God made jealousy as the price you pay for love.

PERIBANEZ (*to* CASILDA). You won't know the meaning of the word.

THE PRIEST. Well I've done my bit. I'm going to sit myself down and enjoy the rest of the day. When you two became one.

PERIBANEZ (*still to* CASILDA). Look at you. I can't believe God has found me such a friend.

THE PRIEST. I'm glad you mention God there – yes – it is God's work. It's He who makes this beautiful face – unmatched in the whole of Toledo.

CASILDA (*to* PERIBANEZ). You can't be as proud as I am to have you. If love was gold, husband, you'd be rich as a King!

PERIBANEZ. You can't outweigh my love Casilda. My mouth will speak my heart and meet you anywhere, everywhere. I'd take the whole of Ocana and lay it at your feet. The entire town and every bit of land, field after field 'til the river's washed through all Portugal and disappeared into the Spanish sea.

What could be more beautiful than you? I can't think of anything. A grove of olive trees, heaving with olives, curling down with fruit? A meadow in early May, first light, when tiny flowers burst open, seeing the world for the first time? Or an apple – shiny and ripe? Thick golden oil, rich and clean in its clay pot? Everything pales, Casilda, next to you. I smell your lips, I can't imagine a better smell. Not even a wine that's been asleep in a tall dark cellar – white, crisp, perfect to drink. I'd compare you to roses if I were a gentleman, but I'm a worker and wine's the thing – but nowhere near as good as you. Could mushroom picking in December, the rain in Spring, the miracle of wheat in August or October's grape-juice come near to the treasure I'll have in my house? Who cares if the summer roasts me or the winter numbs me? I'm complete. I just have to look after this (*Indicates his chest.*) – it's your home – it needs to be worthy of you.

D'you think a Peasant can become a King through the peace in his heart? I think yes. Which means you're a Queen, Casilda. My Queen.

I want to bring you such happiness. Everybody'll wonder how did it happen? How did perfect Casilda turn out to have the Devil's own Luck? That's how happy Heaven will make you, wife, if I have anything to do with it.

CASILDA. Now where do I start? How can I even begin to say everything I feel without my heart breaking open? You make me feel more alive than anything in the world – more than dancing, the music, my pulse, feet racing, drum pounding, the drummer yelling and whooping with all the strength in his throat, my muscles aching from smiling happiness . . . Your voice, the words you choose, lift me more than Midsummer's Day – hearing the cheers come up from the village, smelling lemon verbena and myrtle. What guitar that squeezes my heart could reach me as you do? In your 'how-d'you-do' hat? You mean more to me than my brand new shoes!

You're better than the best banner in the parade, better than the crumbly bread Uncle hands round at Baptisms, better than the Resurrection candle that never goes out. Out of a thousand boys you are the Easter cake covered all over with marzipan chicks and chocolate eggs. No.

She thinks, then she speaks.

You're a young bull in a green field or a clean white shirt folded in a basket of jasmine flowers. You – you're my Pedro. You're you. That's it, I've nothing left to compare you with.

Somebody blows a note or two on their instrument.

THE PRIEST. Right, well I think that's probably enough talk of these loving matters. The youngsters want to dance.

PERIBANEZ (*to their guests*). Please forgive us . . . love makes us rude.

GIL. You carry on!

ANTON. Love 'til you're a complete disgrace!

Music and dancing, including 'Folia' – a dance called Madness.

SINGERS.
    Each lilly that bursts through the earth so proud
    Is speaking of you, of you, of you, of you
    The cliffs that are dripping with melted snow
    Know it's May, it's May, you're married today.
    The river is spilling out over the land
    Blossom's erupting wherever it can
    For Pedro to take his new wife by the hand
    All for you.

    BENITO *enters in the middle of the dancing. He's in a hurry.*

PERIBANEZ. Benito – come and join us!

SINGERS.
    May all of life's blessings fall on you Casilda
    Your hens lay white eggs and your pig fatten well,
    Your cow have three calves and her milk never end
    And the bull, the bull, the bull be your friend.
    All is yours.

BENITO. Anton, you know your beautiful new mare – one of the bulls is going wild out there, he's a mad Spaniard! The wildest we've had for a wedding. Don't know what that suggests about you Pedro, being the bridegroom –

ANTON. What's happened Beni?

BENITO. You know your horse was in the field, well, we've roped the bull finally but it's taken the whole time you were in Church – more than an hour to get the rope round his horns. Old Blas was *dancing* round the field like a Spring lamb trying to rope him, but, your new mare Anton – we couldn't stop him, he was going for anything – you can see what she had for breakfast the size of the hole he's ripped in her side.

ANTON. No!

BENITO. I'm sorry.

ANTON. Oh God. (*To* PERIBANEZ.) Do you mind if I –

PERIBANEZ. No, 'course.

ANTON *hurries out.*

THE PRIEST. It can't get in here can it?

BENITO. It's planning to, by the look on its face.

THE PRIEST. Pedro I think I'll trot up to the terrace for some air.

BENITO. It's still rushing at everything, thin air, despite the rope. A Fury. They're bringing him up to the square now but no-one's dared spike him yet.

COSTANZA. Don't go without a prayer Father.

THE PRIEST. A prayer?

COSTANZA. To protect us!

THE PRIEST. Costanza, believe me, that bull doesn't understand Latin.

THE PRIEST *leaves.*

INES. Yes but God does, doesn't he?

Shouts are heard.

COSTANZA. Oh my God!

INES. Let's go out. You're sure he's tied?

BENITO. I wouldn't go back out if he wasn't.

Everybody goes off to see the bull.

PERIBANEZ. Shall I try and spike him?

CASILDA. He's raging Pedro.

PERIBANEZ. He'll calm quick enough, if you get the spike in his neck. I'd grab his horns and wrestle him down with my hands for you.

CASILDA. Just the thing for a newly married man – to impale yourself on a mad bull's horns . . .

PERIBANEZ. There are better things to do . . .

He moves towards her. A shout of alarm from people outside.

CASILDA. My God what's that?

More voices of panic and organisation.

CASILDA. Something's happened.

PERIBANEZ. They should've left him in the field.

BENITO *enters.*

BENITO. Clear some space here – we need your house.

PERIBANEZ. What's happened?

BENITO (*trying to rearrange the room*). Your wedding may not be the day you sing songs about with grandchildren on your knee, Jesus in Heaven, great hairy bull! I hope you don't find a single blade of grass come April! I hope it's worse for you than August. When you're deranged with jealousy I hope your rival wins the cow and when you're bellowing through the lonely woods your heart in pieces, I hope the stream's bone dry. Damn – I hope you die a rusty, painful death, gotten from behind by some *imbecile* and that you sit down in the dust and turn it red!

PERIBANEZ. What is it Beni?

BENITO. Help me here –

PERIBANEZ. What?

BENITO. They're bringing the Commander in.

PERIBANEZ. The Commander?

BENITO. Your – my – Jesus, our Commander – chief, landlord, governor, prince –

CASILDA. What happened?

BENITO. He was riding down to the square on his red bay – swishing black tail, sparkling silver bridle. He sees the bull charging back and forth on its rope and, without a thought, so valiant, takes up his lance, kicks the bay and vaults her into action. Thundering down past all the people towards the mad bull and . . . the bull runs in front of him, the horse's legs get tangled in the rope and, dah! He's off. Fell straight on his back, a hell of a fall. God forgive us, not good at all. Here he is now – look, like a babe in arms.

Enter the COMMANDER, *unconscious, with* ANTON, GIL, *and some other villagers.*

ANTON. Is the Priest still here? We might need him.

PERIBANEZ. The terrace Benito – go and get him.

BENITO. Right.

PERIBANEZ. Quickly.

BENITO *goes.*

ANTON. We need to get someone from his house –

GIL. I think he's dead.

ANTON. My heart's kicking my ribs.

ANTON *goes to get some of the* COMMANDER'*s people.* EVERYBODY ELSE *leaves, not wanting to implicate themselves in the tragedy of the dying* COMMANDER.

PERIBANEZ. Because of us. This is my fault. The marriage bull's the groom isn't it? I'll have to leave Ocana. We'll have to go away.

CASILDA. I think he moved. Run Pedro – get water quick.

PERIBANEZ *goes to get water.*

CASILDA (*to the* COMMANDER). It's coming soon. The water. (*The* COMMANDER *doesn't stir.*) How could this happen to you? You're the flower of Spain. You made the Arabs too scared to sleep at night. How many hearts has your sword sliced into? (*She takes a good look at him.*) Look at your hands – fighter's hands. What a man. How did a rope stop you – when no-one else has been fast enough, or sure enough. I can feel your strength from here. And I'm watching your life ease out of you. Death slips in with an old bull's leash on our wedding day. What for? Thieves die by the rope, not soldiers. (*Still looking at him.*) Don't die Commander. (*Calling him quietly.*) Commander? Commander of Ocana?

COMMANDER. Who's calling me?

CASILDA. Thank you Lord.

COMMANDER. Ah, who are you?

CASILDA. Sir, me. I mean, only me. You're so very welcome here. You're not to worry about anything. You chased after a mad bull, that's all. Please be at home. I know it's not like your home but . . .

COMMANDER. Are you an angel? Everything I've ever seen that's beautiful.

CASILDA. You're seeing visions Sir. You're alive and –

COMMANDER. How? I died, there on the ground, and just as I knew I was dead I opened my eyes and – are you here for me? (*The* COMMANDER *reaches out and tries to hold on to* CASILDA.)

CASILDA. Sir! (*She manages to prise his hands off her.*) You're alive, and if you're pleased to find yourself here, in my house, then you must congratulate me as it's only been mine since today.

COMMANDER. Ah. (*He supports himself so he can sit upright.*) You're . . . the Bride?

CASILDA. Yes. I'm sorry to say, if our celebrations have caused you harm.

COMMANDER. So you're married?

CASILDA. To the best man in the world, yes.

COMMANDER. That can't often be said by a beautiful woman.

CASILDA. Well I've got the Devil's luck.

COMMANDER. What's your name?

CASILDA. Casilda your Honour.

COMMANDER (*aside*). (I've never seen such vivid grace – married to some dirty-finger-nailed farm hand). I think the 'best man in the world' has the Devil's own luck. (*Aside.*) (Diamond!)

CASILDA. He's not the lucky one – I am Commander. There's no contest.

COMMANDER. You could be wife to any man, Casilda.

CASILDA *laughs.* COMMANDER *watches her. They look at each other.*

Enter PERIBANEZ *with some water.*

PERIBANEZ. I don't know where the Priest's gone.

CASILDA. It's alright – Lord Don Fadrique – is better.

PERIBANEZ. I can see. Thank God.

COMMANDER. Your wife has healing hands.

LUJAN *and* FLOREZ, *the* COMMANDER*'s serving boy, appear.*

FLOREZ. Is that him talking?

LUJAN. Sir, are you . . . ? We've brought the travelling chair Sir.

COMMANDER. Well take it away again – I don't need it.

LUJAN. Praise the Lord!

COMMANDER (*to* PERIBANEZ *and* CASILDA). When I'm fully recovered I shan't forget my debt to you.

PERIBANEZ. If I could offer you my health Commander, I would.

COMMANDER. I'm sure.

COMMANDER *stands but falls again, finding he needs help with walking.*

LUJAN. How are you Sir?

COMMANDER. Filled with hunger.

FLOREZ. Shall I arrange for an early supper Sir?

COMMANDER. Forget it.

LUJAN. I meant the fall – how are you?

COMMANDER. Somewhere between Heaven and Hell.

Exit all except CASILDA *and* PERIBANEZ.

PERIBANEZ. He seems alright.

CASILDA. Thank God.

PERIBANEZ. Not the best omen on our wedding day.

CASILDA. I think he'll be fine. It could even be lucky for us –
he may help us one day.

Pause.

PERIBANEZ. Thanks to you, and your healing hands.

I want you. You have the key to the house now, and to me.
Ask me anything you like. I want to sink my troubles in you
my lovely Casilda.

CASILDA. Teach me how to be a good Wife.

PERIBANEZ. A good Wife? A good Wife. Must . . . adore her
husband . . .

CASILDA. That's A, what's B?

PERIBANEZ. B? She must be o*be*dient, of course . . . are you
listening?

CASILDA. I'm listening . . . C?

PERIBANEZ. C means she's *c*lean and . . . *d*ocile, for D. She's
an *e*xcellent cook and she'll steer clear of mad *e*xcesses!
*F*aithful, *G*odly. *H*onourable, and my house will be
*i*lluminated by her. J. Be *j*ust and K, *k*iss me, which leads
to – easy – *l*ove me. Be my *M*istress, and the *M*aster of our
*n*aughty children. N and O together – not many women
know this one – '*no*', to wayward requests. Rather you'll be
*p*ensive and *q*uick to see trouble – using your *r*eason (you'll
be very reasonable). S means you'll always *s*eek my
approval and T, T is a good Wife *t*reads carefully. U, '*us*'. V
– *v*irtuous, W, *w*illing, e*x*tremely understanding, *y*ielding . . .
and don't ever get jealous or it will de*z*troy our sky-like
tranquility! And there we are. That's it. How to become a
perfect Wife with a simple A – Z, and make your husband
happy as a Prince.

CASILDA. I think I can learn your ABC but I've got a spelling book for you too.

PERIBANEZ. Go on. Let me learn from you.

CASILDA. Sit still and listen. The first letter means you mustn't be *a*bove me. B is always *b*e nice to me. C says good husbands are good *c*ompanions and D – *d*on't ever forget about me. You must be *e*asy to talk to and *f*un. Be *g*allant on my behalf, always be *h*onest, and – repeat after me and every night after that, '*I* thank you for my delicious supper Casilda' and '*I* love you Casilda'. Don't make me *j*ealous or it will *k*ill me. Don't *l*ose your head, be open-*m*inded, N – that's for *n*onsense, which I simply won't put up with and '*O*h'! is for surprises, which I hope I'll have *p*lenty of. Take care of me like a *p*arent does – and however many people are *q*ueuing for your attention always put me first. R is for *r*omance, you can *s*erve me with S, be *t*rue to me and never *u*njust, give me *v*alleys full of presents and oh I've missed out W but never mind because X, this is as far as I'm going because X is for this – (*She opens wide her arms and legs.*) – which is how I hope to die, with you.

An embrace.

PERIBANEZ. I promise to learn your alphabet by heart. What else can I do for you?

CASILDA. I want to ask you something. But maybe now's not the time . . .

PERIBANEZ. Ask me.

CASILDA. I wondered, because we've just got married, you know the festival in August, I've always wanted to go to Toledo and see the virgin Mary in the procession –

PERIBANEZ. Let's do it.

CASILDA. Pedro really? That's G for gallant. (*She kisses his hands.*)

PERIBANEZ. Invite your cousins too. Why not? Let's take a full cart and make a holiday of it.

CASILDA. Really? Can we really?

PERIBANEZ. We can really, and will really. And Toledo'll be lucky to have us!

But tell me again, what was in your spelling book for 'X' . . . ?

CASILDA. Um . . ,

He kisses her fully.

Scene Two

The COMMANDER*'s house.*

COMMANDER. Leonardo! Tell Lujan to get in here, I want to ride today!

LEONARDO. I have done. He was preoccupied with the horses.

COMMANDER. Well tell him again.

LEONARDO. Yes Sir.

COMMANDER. Go on then.

LEONARDO (*aside*). (August. Two and a half months since his fall. Ten whole weeks of nothing being right. Not in pain, but won't take pleasure. Fit but floundering, sighs all day. Some commander – in love with a peasant. Garrotte me if he isn't.)

LEONARDO *exits.*

COMMANDER. You hooded beauty. So alive, so alert. I burn at the thought of you, Casilda. You're snow and sunshine. Bright, light. Red – like spreading dawn. Uh. Who's this man, who's made an August of your heart and reaped it all? I want it – what he has. Peasant. To feel your hand on me, Casilda, absolute and certain, your palm on my face. The acute gentleness of your eye watching me without fear. As if I were a rare and spiky rose. Wanting to be picked by

you. Your firm hold, your cautious fingers. A ripe field, you
are. Primed. Ready. To yield crops of soft fruit, year after
year, 'til your house is littered with our children.

Enter LUJAN.

LUJAN. Sorry Sir, the horse was thirsty, but if you're sure
you're ready to ride again I've –

COMMANDER. Get these boots on.

LUJAN *begins putting the* COMMANDER*'s boots on.
When he's only half way through the job,* COMMANDER
kicks him away and paces round the room.

LUJAN. Are you alright Sir?

COMMANDER. I can't – . Still ringing from a – .

LUJAN. Is it the girl Sir?

COMMANDER. Yes. Yes Lujan. The girl. I keep going to her
in my mind, like a moth to light.

LUJAN *gently proceeds to finish putting the*
COMMANDER*'s boots on.*

What do they like, these peasants? Would it arouse
suspicion if I offered her something – in return for their
hospitality?

LUJAN. Well, no . . . that's what I'd do Sir – but cautiously.
Approach the husband first. Not that he's an idiot, but no-
one's immune to presents and, well, then you'd have him
you see – he'd be in your debt.

COMMANDER. Yes, yes. Good. What should I give him?

LUJAN. Mules. A couple of mules. Better than giving him the
whole of Ocana. And maybe – some earrings for the lady
Wife? Or – shoes . . . D'you know the tale of Angelica and
Carlos?

The battlefield heaves with meaty carnage
For fair Angelica's hand in marriage:
Malgesi thrusts while Roldan charges
Ferragut swoops, the battle rages,

Poor great Sacripante is torn apart
The heroes at war for the lady's heart.

But back among the Cypress trees
Carlos, there upon his knees
Presents her with a pair of shoes
And with this gift the lady woos.
Thus fair Angelica for thirteen moons
Gives him all love's sighs and swoons.

Generosity Sir, in the material sense, that's the nub. And it attends to discretion. Favours are good, but they're like a beacon – "Over here, the Commander's in love!" No Sir, simple generosity goes an awfully long way, quietly, like the Gods.

COMMANDER. That's enough. You're right. Let generosity do the talking.

LUJAN. You won't be disappointed Sir. It can flatten mountains, it can fill in seas . . .

COMMANDER. You've said enough.

We might have to take a little look at your duties to me and reassess.

LUJAN. Anything I can do for you Sir you need just ask. I've no shoes or earrings . . . but all I can do, I will. I'm all yours.

COMMANDER. I need help. (*The* COMMANDER *is flooded with disquiet and unfulfilled longing.*)

LUJAN. You're in a mess aren't you? Generosity will pave your way Sir, don't you worry.

COMMANDER. That poet knew his salt from his water. Lucky old Carlos.

Mules then Lujan, the most beautiful mules you can find.

LUJAN. You plant that gold, the mules will plough his heart and, trust me Sir, Love will be your harvest.

Scene Three

PERIBANEZ' *house.*

CASILDA. I hope we don't miss anything.

INES. We won't – look at the weather!

COSTANZA. Blas was boasting how it only takes him six hours in summer, and his horse is really old.

INES. It's flat all the way once we're down the hill.

COSTANZA. What are you wearing Ines?

INES (*indicates herself*). D'you like it?

COSTANZA. Oh. I've brought my bodice with silver threading with me . . .

INES. Lovely – with a bit of ripe peach peeping out..

CASILDA. Well it's the red velvet for me, now I'm a married woman..

COSTANZA. I wish I had – you know that blue skirt that Anton's wife lent me?

INES. Yes – that's nice on you.

COSTANZA. Well Menga said the skirt didn't go with my face, so she made me give it to her.

INES. You'd eat your mother if someone told you to! I know who'd lend you a really beautiful skirt..

COSTANZA. Who?

INES. Casilda.

CASILDA. Oh, you can borrow the white one if you like. (CASILDA *catches* INES' *eye.*) Or the green one with pleats?

INES *and* CASILDA *smirk at each other.*

COSTANZA. Are you serious? I mean, that's your special skirt – what would Pedro say?

CASILDA. He'd be happy to see it again – it's his favourite.

COSTANZA. I – oh – thank you. (COSTANZA *is blushing*.)

INES (*to* CASILDA *with a knowing look*). I hope you've washed it. So tell us. What's it like? Does he still love you?

CASILDA. What d'you expect? We're still eating the wedding cake!

COSTANZA. Does he do lots of fantastic things to you?

INES. Costanza!

COSTANZA. I didn't mean . . . I didn't mean. I mean – how does he love you?

CASILDA. How doesn't he? I'm light-headed thinking about it!

INES. Come on, you can't stop there.

CASILDA. Every day in our new lives, just as the glow worms come out, Pedro comes home, sweaty from his day's work, hungry for supper. I know he's on his way before he gets here. I drop my work, put everything aside for the next day, head to the door and there he is. He hurls himself off the horse. I throw myself into his arms and stay there wrapped in him – for so long the horse starts kicking and neighing, getting hungrier and hungrier. Pedro says, 'I have to feed this lot', but he takes my face and kisses me so gently, and says 'then I'm all yours'. He gets the hay, I get the barley. The animals munch away, we sieve and stir the grain together and, we usually forget what we're supposed to be doing. I love it in the stable. There's nowhere too cold or dark for love. But then our warm house calls us. The saucepan rattles and the onion and garlic ooze their juice. It's music. Makes me want to dance. He watches me, beaming, as I lay the table – always a fresh tablecloth and our plates with the carnations on. And the smell . . . I swear even the Commander doesn't eat better! I take such care with his food, letting it steam until it's perfect, feeling his eyes on me. And when we sit down to eat, after the day he's had, before he's even swallowed his first mouthful, he chooses the best bits and feeds them to me. That's how we eat. Then if we've got any olives I fetch them and we salt

our tongues. If there's no olives we're happy anyway.
Completely. And, maybe it's superstitious, but always when
we've finished we hold hands and thank God for our good
fortune and – then it's bed, where I wish we could stay
forever. Until Dawn arrives, unwelcome, and calls us, 'Get
up, get to work, begin another day!'

INES. I hate you.

COSTANZA. You're so lucky!

INES. Here he is, famous husband . . .

PERIBANEZ *enters.*

PERIBANEZ. Well the cart's packed but, I'm sorry Casilda, it
doesn't look very festive. Manrique's turned up with some
carpet and a big banner on his cart – it's unrecognizable
from the dung-heap it normally carries.

CASILDA. What if we borrow a banner?

INES. You could ask the Commander.

COSTANZA. Yes, ask the Commander!

PERIBANEZ. No, no. Who else could we borrow one from?

INES. Go on – you helped him!

COSTANZA. You saved his life!

CASILDA. It's worth asking. Isn't it?

PERIBANEZ. Maybe. Why not? (*Happy agreement from the*
GIRLS.) If we're going let's go in style.

INES. Time for us to get changed then girls!

COSTANZA. I thought..?

INES. I was joking! You think I'm going to Toledo in this?

CASILDA. Pedro, while you're there, why don't you ask him?

PEDRO. Hmm?

CASILDA. If he has a hat you could borrow?

PERIBANEZ. A hat?

CASILDA. Why not?

PERIBANEZ. I don't want a big feathered thing on my head –
do I look like a tree?

COSTANZA *and* INES *laugh.*

It's the beginning of the end that – a feathered hat! You'll
want pearl earrings next!

He goes off grumbling to make the GIRLS *laugh.*
CASILDA *watches him go. Before he goes off he returns
quickly and brings* CASILDA *to him for a kiss.*

Scene Four

The COMMANDER*'s house.*

COMMANDER. What a pair.

LUJAN. They are exquisite. I can safely say in my extensive
dealings with mules – I've never seen finer.

COMMANDER. So just the earrings.

LUJAN. The dealer reckons they'll be turning three come
Harvest and I reckon he's right. They're saddle-bearers too
– no sulking at the weight.

COMMANDER. We can't just present him with mules and
jewellery. He'll smell a rat, surely.

LUJAN. Call him in, grease him with your gratitude. Show
him how you've recovered.

It makes me laugh that you've chosen me as your secretary
for matters of the heart!

COMMANDER. Don't let it. If it were a high-born lady I were
pursuing I'd have Leonardo do it. Who'd procure me
diamonds, jewels, pearls, soft damask, the Arabian phoenix,
anything the lady wanted. But you, my mule-man. Casilda

is a peasant. I have to approach her through a peasant. You deal with my love in a language that it understands.

LUJAN. Of course Sir. I didn't mean – .

As you say, she's a diamond set in lead. Making her a slightly delirious choice if I may say so Sir. But you're choosing your plan of action wisely.

LEONARDO *enters.*

LEONARDO. Peribanez is here.

COMMANDER. Who?

LEONARDO. Peribanez.

COMMANDER. Say again.

LEONARDO. Pedro Ibanez is here, wanting to see you. I believe you've met. A highly respected farmer, recently married, and popular. Should the peasants ever rebel, God forbid, in Ocana, they'd probably choose Peribanez as their leader. An honourable man, Sir, even 'though he's a peasant.

LUJAN. You're looking a bit unwell Sir.

COMMANDER. I'm in love with a woman and her husband turns up. It makes me unwell.

LUJAN. Shall I send him away?

COMMANDER. No, I want to see him. A maid carries the essence of her lady – why not her husband? I want to see her beauty in his eye.

Enter PERIBANEZ.

PERIBANEZ. Give me your generous feet. (*He goes to kneel.*)

COMMANDER. Pedro, you're welcome in my house. A guest of honour. Give me your arms. (COMMANDER *embraces him instead.*)

PERIBANEZ. Sir, I – don't deserve this. I'm only a farmer.

COMMANDER. Don't be modest Pedro. I understand you're an exemplary figure in Ocana, you've never defaulted on your taxes, and you saved my life – where would I be

without you? What can I offer you? Name the favour
Peribanez.

PERIBANEZ. I was recently married – you were there that
day. My wife, Casilda, wants to go to Toledo for the
festival. 'Though I'm a working man I understand what
Gentlemen do for their ladies. I've said I'll take her, and her
cousins. But I only have woven rugs at home – nothing to
decorate the cart with. We don't have banners or hangings
or anything with a coat of arms. Could I borrow a banner
for our cart? Please forgive my clumsy speech and ignorant
request. I – it's out of love that I ask.

COMMANDER. Are you happy Pedro?

PERIBANEZ. Am I? I'm happier than any man alive. I've an
open-hearted, honourable and not bad-looking wife who
loves me. I don't know if it's as much as I love her, but it's
more than I've ever been loved before. I couldn't ask for
anything greater.

COMMANDER. Splendid. That's how marriage should be.
(*Calls off.*) Florez! (*Young FLOREZ enters.*) Fetch the fresh
arrival from Morocco. (*To* PERIBANEZ.) A beautiful piece
of carpet, (*To* FLOREZ.) and eight silk hangings with my
Arms on.

FLOREZ *makes to leave.*

Wait! Since this is my chance to repay him for taking me in
to his home, rousing me from the dead, bring the two mules
I bought for long distance travel – (COMMANDER *looks
at* FLOREZ, *who looks confused.*) – and give them to our
guest – (FLOREZ *makes to go.*) – *and*, if the smith has
finished the job, offer the new earrings to his kind wife.

FLOREZ *exits, a little uncertain of his instructions.*

PERIBANEZ. I'm overwhelmed. Sir, this kindness is
unnecessary. If I kissed the ground a thousand times I
couldn't repay you for this rare generosity. My wife and I
have always worked your land and served you with our
hearts – but now we're your slaves.

COMMANDER. Take him out the front Leonardo.

LEONARDO. If you'd like to follow me.

PERIBANEZ *follows* LEONARDO *out.*

COMMANDER. What do you say to that Lujan?

LUJAN. Well. That was good timing!

COMMANDER. Listen to me. Go to the stables and saddle the chestnut stallion. I'm going after her, in disguise.

LUJAN. To Toledo? That's half a day's ride and you've only just –

COMMANDER. I'm well enough! Peasant that she is she's haunting me and I'm going to haunt her back. If I see her it might – this fire here in my soul might – cool.

Scene Five

In the empty Cathedral in Toledo. The CONSTABLE *is speaking with the* KING, *accompanied by* ARCEO.

CONSTABLE. Toledo welcomes you as a father. To receive you at such a time, the evening before our lady's Assumption, doubles our pleasure.

INES, COSTANZA, CASILDA *and* PERIBANEZ *enter, with the* COMMANDER *close behind them.*

INES. There he is! Oh my God – I can't believe it's him!

COSTANZA. He's so handsome!

INES. I've seen King Henry III!

CASILDA. Third? Looks First-rate to me.

CONSTABLE. Might your Majesty grace us with your presence in our procession tomorrow?

KING. How could I miss it? This Christian festival at such a time shines as a glittering crown of Castille.

I have a request for your Virgin on behalf of all honest
Spaniards, for her prayers in my Campaign against the Arab
in our country.

CONSTABLE. I can't think but she must oblige you Sir.

INES. Who's he talking to, with the straight back?

PERIBANEZ. Must be the Constable, at least.

CASILDA. Kings are really made of meat and bone?

INES. What did you think?

CASILDA. Damask or velvet.

COSTANZA. You didn't really did you?

COMMANDER (*aside*). (I'm like a shadow. Too close – I'll be
seen. By the King even.)

CONSTABLE. As to your other request. The nobility want
nothing more than to see the Arab defeated and to that end
have agreed to support your campaign. We can offer a
thousand men from greater Toledo and forty thousand new
gold coins.

KING. Thank you for this news. I knew Toledo wouldn't let
me down. You'll see how grateful I am to the Nobility of
your city.

The KING *leaves, with the* CONSTABLE.

INES. Oh no, he's away.

COSTANZA. Don't go! I couldn't even see if he was a blonde
or a red-head!

INES. Costanza, Kings are like small miracles – every time
you see them they change colour.

COSTANZA. Really?

COMMANDER (*aside*). (Thank God he's gone.)

LUJAN *and the* PAINTER *enter.*

LUJAN. There he is.

PAINTER. Where?

LUJAN. Ssh! Sir – here's the painter.

COMMANDER. Welcome.

PAINTER. Happy to be of service Sir.

COMMANDER. Did you bring your paints?

PAINTER. Brought paper and water colours, thinking ahead.

COMMANDER. You see the woman in the middle there? I
    want you to paint her, without her knowing you're doing it.

PAINTER. Could be tricky – I'll do my best. I'm sure I'll
    catch her likeness.

COMMANDER. There's more work if you do. If I like your
    sketch I'll commission a full scale oil painting, d'you
    understand?

PAINTER. D'you want the whole lady Sir?

COMMANDER. From her waist up, but be precise! Every
    bead and button, just as she is.

LUJAN. Looks like they're staying here.

PAINTER. That's me to work then. (*Gets out his equipment.*)

PERIBANEZ. Look at the candles Casilda.

INES. Did you know there's bulls in the square tonight?

CASILDA. I'm glad we're out the way. I like it here.

COMMANDER. Painter I want the sky in the picture, a
    meadow full of flowers, put it all in.

PAINTER. Right. She's very beautiful.

COMMANDER (*watching* CASILDA). She radiates – beauty.

    A rare beauty.

LUJAN (*to the* PAINTER). Likes his meat raw.

PAINTER. It's dark in here – I'm afraid I'm losing the light.

COMMANDER. How? Those steady eyes –
    You see stars, maybe, spreading pale rays,
    I see suns, setting my world ablaze.

ACT TWO

Scene One

A committee meeting – Ocaña.

THE PRIEST. That's what I think!

GIL. But it's a guild Father, please sit down – we need to put it into writing, make it official, then take a vote on it.

ANTON. With only four of us here?

THE PRIEST. Everyone knew it was today.

BENITO. No one came to the festival – why would they come today?

THE PRIEST. And why didn't they come to the festival? We did everything we could, but if the heart of it's not right you see, if the centre's rotten –

GIL. Festivals are springing up all over the place with fantastic shows of devotion. We'll be a disgrace to Spain if we don't do something soon. Why are we so afraid of spending money?

THE PRIEST. It's obvious why. If I weren't such a temperate man I'd call it pinch-fisted.

BENITO. Is that temperance?

PERIBANEZ *enters.*

PERIBANEZ. Sorry I'm late, I meant to be here earlier. I hope I'm in time to be some use.

BENITO. Never too late Pedro – God keep you. (*The* OTHERS *mumble their greetings to him.*) 'Though we could have done with you before now.

PERIBANEZ. I'm sorry.

THE PRIEST. Sit yourself down here, Pedro, next to me.

GIL. Where have you been?

THE PRIEST. On holiday! Taking my niece to Toledo. Her very first time. And how was the festival? Of course I could never leave Ocana in August, otherwise I'd have taken her myself before now.

PERIBANEZ. We've only been back a day.

ANTON. Any good?

PERIBANEZ. Magnificent. The Virgin – she must've been painted by saints and angels. She's luminous. They've surely seen the real one up on her sky-lit throne. Her face is all light. The procession too – they know how to do it in Toledo. With the King himself adding to the occasion – we saw him twice.

THE PRIEST. Did you now?

GIL. The King huh?

PERIBANEZ. He's gathering an army – the leaders of Alcantara and Calatrava were there, but I didn't see them. It's a big Campaign. The Arabs won't be drinking in the town squares much longer. I'm sure our men won't get a warm welcome either.

GIL. Well we've missed you.

PERIBANEZ. I thought we'd be back the next day for San Roque – I've never missed our festival before, but, I'm sorry Father, uncle, I couldn't bring Casilda away. She loved it – especially the Virgin. Anyway, enough of my life, what's the trouble?

GIL. The festival. And seeing you come in there Pedro you're the only man who can heave us from this ditch. I want Pedro to take over the chairmanship, I've had enough. No one listens to me anyway.

BENITO. I was just thinking the same.

GIL. Thank you for that!

ANTON. It's a good idea Gil. Father? Shall I – I'd like to propose Pedro as new chairman.

BENITO (*raising his hand*). No-one's going to object to that I presume?

GIL (*raising his hand*). Then it's up to Pedro to make sure we've got all we need for next festival.

THE PRIEST *also raises his hand.*

PERIBANEZ. Gentlemen it's kind of you to offer – I'm honoured – but I'm a newly-married man, I can't! My time is Casilda's time now. (*He looks at them all with their hands still in the air.*) Gentlemen, please. (*They keep their hands up.*) Oh, how can I . . . ? For our Saint. It'll inspire me to more devotion. Yes, all right, I'll be chairman this year.

They finally drop their hands, satisfied.

THE PRIEST. There's a boy.

PERIBANEZ. So. What's the story?

THE PRIEST. It's quite simple – we need a new statue, a big one. One that catches the eye, you know? A real event-stealer.

PERIBANEZ. Right. Good idea. Gil?

GIL. Father's right. Our San Roque is passed it and, let's face it, he's too small.

PERIBANEZ. Anton?

ANTON. His dog's peeling, half his bread's missing, the angel's split right the way up – and there's something not right about being blessed by a hand that's missing two fingers. I say let's get another one – one they really can pray to.

PERIBANEZ. Beni – what do you say?

BENITO. That you and Anton should take yourselves off to Toledo, find a painter, get his fingers put back on and get our San Roque done up. It's not right spending money we haven't got on a bigger, better version when we already have a saint. Is the church going to pay? He's big enough.

THE PRIEST. Well.

PERIBANEZ. It's true – funds aren't flowing. We'd have to find the money from somewhere . . . And what would we do with this one? We couldn't throw him out. How would we get him to town?

ANTON. Strap him on to the donkey.

BENITO. Or one of your new mules . . .

ANTON. If we wrap him in a blanket he should be safe.

PERIBANEZ. Gil?

GIL. It's – a possible plan.

PERIBANEZ. Father?

THE PRIEST. Well I can see how the tide is moving. (*To* PERIBANEZ.) And you were just saying yourself how the Virgin in Toledo made the festival for you. But you're the chairman now, and if that's the decision the guild wants to take then who am I to stop it? End of the meeting then. And the beginning of the death of the Ocanan festival of San Roque, patron saint of plagues and diseases.

BENITO. Before we conclude for the day can I just say I'm not skirting my responsibilities. I'll pay my share. If the Guild decides to make a San Roque the size of the Commander's house I'll pitch in, whatever it takes.

THE PRIEST. Lucky for you the Guild's decided to keep costs down then. (*To* ANTON *and* PERIBANEZ.) You'd better be on your way – get your prize mule ready – saddle the horses, say goodbye to your wives. Tell Casilda I'll look in on her tomorrow.

PERIBANEZ. I can't go now – I've just come back. I can't do it 'til after harvest.

BENITO. A blanket won't keep him safe in September.

ANTON. It's true Pedro, we can't risk the rain.

PERIBANEZ. But . . .

GIL. If you go tomorrow and you're lucky with a painter you'd be back by Thursday – they can make a start without you.

PERIBANEZ. I can't miss three whole days of harvest.

THE PRIEST. Casilda won't like it at all.

ANTON. If we went right now, with God's grace we could make it by nightfall.

BENITO. You could.

Pause.

PERIBANEZ. I need to go and break the news to Casilda.

ANTON. I'll take the Saint, meet you up at the house in an hour?

PERIBANEZ. I can't believe I'm doing this. Walking out on Casilda at harvest time! What kind of husband is that? Anton? San Roque calls. I'll count the moments 'til I'm home with my Casilda.

Scene Two

The COMMANDER's *house.*

LEONARDO. It's Ines, her cousin – her *not* recently-married cousin. If it's any use to have her on side –

COMMANDER. Tell me.

LEONARDO. As soon as they were back from Toledo I took it on myself to draw her in. She's the dawn to Casilda's sun – she's the siesta – softer, shadier, more accessible. So yesterday I spent the day walking up and down her road as often as I could. You have to have your wits about you, they've always got an eye out for each other these people. Until the evening when, luck would have it, there was a dance so I could speak to her. And there she was, turned out in her peasant girl's best. I told her how glorious she looked. I softened my eyes, I looked miserable, I spoke meaningfully about love, and children – that pumped the colour high in her cheeks. Sweet. Like a ripe tomato.

I looked broken-hearted when we said goodnight. She was
embarrassed but today I happened to bump into her again
on her way to the threshing floor and told her how I hadn't
slept for the pain in my heart, and that was it. Twenty four
hours. She'll heal my aching heart. Not before I'd given her
the 'marry me' line to be fair – she did have doubts – but
I told her, I like this bit, that if you agreed then you could
be the one to marry us. As if you're a Priest! She lit up at
that. It must be you or we couldn't do it, I said, because
you're like a father to me – no offence. And she had to keep
it quiet 'til I've spoken to you . . . So Sir, I'm confident that
if we need her help –

COMMANDER. I wish it were that easy. Casilda's inhuman.
She's like a rock, solid against the tide.

LEONARDO. No advance then?

COMMANDER. I followed her like breath on her neck all the
way – not easy – and seized my chance when she turned in
the procession. I lowered my cape from my face and looked
directly at her. Her face was horror. I could have been
Death. It flushed with colour then blanched – completely
drained of life – anger and disdain scrawled across it. It was
a simple appeal – I showed her how I felt. But Leonardo,
that arrogance! I want her more, every muscle in me's
straining for her.

I know it's madness, but I got her portrait done. Caught her
proud spirit in paint.

LEONARDO. Good likeness?

COMMANDER. Yes. I've commissioned an oil. You're
expected in Toledo to fetch it home.

LEONARDO. Not Lujan?

COMMANDER. No, I want him here. And you'll know how to
get it back safely. The painter's working quickly because I
need it. I have to have her somehow. If I can't get my hands
on the original I'll have the canvas one – always in sight.
Hang her where I want her.

LEONARDO. But a painting's a painting. You're fixed on the
    girl and you'll carry on with this suffering until you've got
    her. Look, give me a day, let me talk to Ines. Casilda knows
    you're after her and isn't budging so we have to try the back
    route. Leave it to me. If it doesn't work I'll go to Toledo
    and get your picture.

COMMANDER. If Ines can persuade her to meet me then
    Leonardo – whatever I have is yours.

Enter LUJAN *dressed as a farm-hand.*

LUJAN. Are you alone Sir?

LEONARDO. Evidently. (*Aside*.) (Lap-dog.)

COMMANDER. My mule-man. Yes. Apart from Leonardo.

LUJAN. Guess what?

COMMANDER. You've got good news? Please God it's good.

LUJAN. As from today I am officially employed by Pedro
    Ibanez.

LEONARDO. What as?

LUJAN. I dressed up as a reaper and I went to ask him for
    work – never judge an orange by its skin eh? And from
    tonight I'm sleeping in his house!

COMMANDER. Why can't I be a reaper?

LUJAN. We leave for work at dawn but Sir, you have the
    whole night before then.

COMMANDER. What d'you mean?

LUJAN. He's gone to Toledo again on some business, leaving
    Casilda on her own. Which I suspect he might regret. We
    sleep right by the door so on a signal from you I can open
    up and lead you straight to her room!

COMMANDER. Lujan, Lujan, how can I ever repay you?

LUJAN. I'm sure you know best how Sir.

COMMANDER. What's his business in Toledo? The joy of
    sheer good luck. We've got Pedro out the way, you on the

other side of the door. He didn't recognize you? I feel
hopeful. For the first time in weeks, there's hope. Did you
look inside the house?

LUJAN. I was even introduced to you know who – in her
room.

COMMANDER. You were in her room? Aren't you scarred?
I'm on fire just thinking of it. What did she say, what was
she doing?

LUJAN. Sewing. Nothing fancy – just leather, blue leather
with a trim of yellow-gold. But you know how with that
kind of braid there's normally tassels?

COMMANDER. Yes . . .

LUJAN. Well there were no tassels. Just plain. Like the corners
had been cut off.

LEONARDO. How interesting.

LUJAN. But do you know what was on the walls?

COMMANDER. No.

LUJAN. It may be because 'August's wind gets under the
skin', or maybe they fancy themselves gentlemen now that
they've had you visit them – although you were
unconscious at the time – but anyway I thought no, they're
hung up in surrender to your love, waving the white flag as
it were.

COMMANDER. What d'you mean?

LUJAN. Sir your Arms are all over her walls.

COMMANDER. Are they? Mounted in triumph – showing
how she's conquered me. But I'm alive – a piece of me lives
in her presence.

You'd better go – don't be seen here. Dear God I need to
get myself ready – wait for night to come. And reproach
me, no doubt, when she does.

LUJAN. Will Leonardo come with you?

LEONARDO. Or am I going to Toledo . . . ?

COMMANDER. That can wait. You need your friends beside you when a bull's been spiked. (*To* LUJAN.) Go on, get going!

Scene Three

PERIBANEZ' *house.*

CASILDA. What can I do to make you stay?

INES. Swap lives with me? Don't be cross, you know what my parents are like, they think I still cry when I bang my knees!

CASILDA. I'll get a message to them, they won't be worried – it's already late.

INES. Oh – go on then, you horrible cousin. Tell them whatever you like!

CASILDA. You don't know how much it means to me – horrible friend.

INES. You. You've turned soft. You've got used to having someone in your bed. But just have a look at these arms (*She shows* CASILDA *her muscles.*) I'm a sorry replacement for perfect Pedro, Casilda. At least you know what a man looks like in the dark – if anyone comes in here I'll run screaming!

CASILDA. I'm not scared of that. Anyway the men are sleeping by the door.

INES. Well if you don't want my muscles . . . am I just here to keep you company in case you can't sleep?

CASILDA. Yes.

INES. Right. You're not worried about Pedro are you? Jealous of him going to Toledo with Anton?

CASILDA. When we were in the procession – (*She stops.*) It's when I can't sleep. Doubt is like air, it creeps in, it doesn't matter where from – it can be from anywhere.

INES. Oh! I always thought it came from Medina . . .

She starts to sing:

The beautiful girls are,
All in Medina,
What's in the air there,
That makes them so fair?

CASILDA. They're pretty nice in Toledo too . . .

INES. Not as nice as you blossom.

CASILDA. Come on, let's go up, the earlies are coming in.

The HARVEST WORKERS *begin to arrive.*

LLORENTE. Bed. Dawn's waiting round the corner.

MENDO. I can smell it already. This'll do me. (MENDO
*makes himself a bed on the floor and wraps himself in his
cape.*)

CASILDA. I need to lock the back door.

INES. Tell Sancho to watch the orchard – it's scary at night.

CASILDA. I'll send him round to your mum's first.

INES *goes up to the bedroom,* CASILDA *goes out to the
back yard.*

LLORENTE. Mrs Pedro'll want us in quickly tonight 'coz he's
away. And out quick in the morning no doubt.

BENITO *and* CHAPARRO *enter.*

BENITO. I'm up the hill tomorrow. Aargh.

CHAPARRO. Lucky you.

MENDO. I don't like this new system. Counting every
niggling piece of corn.

CHAPARRO. Good work always shines through Mendo.
(*Making his bed.*) So who's got a song?

Someone starts one on the guitar.

BENITO. Nah! I'll die if I hear that one more time. (BENITO
has found his space on the floor by now.) God save me what

a grumpy tired old knacker I am. I have to give up this
work, I've done my time.

LLORENTE. Oh sleep. (*Lying down.*) If I woke up four times
next year I'd be a happy man.

Enter HELIPE *and* LUJAN.

HELIPE. Shove up boys.

MENDO. No, not Helipe.

HELIPE. Next to you then Mendo?

LUJAN. D'you think you could all move up a bit and I'll
squeeze in by the door?

CHAPARRO. 'Course. Budge up Helipe.

BENITO. You can keep the draught out. You got a song for us –
that we haven't heard before?

LUJAN. I've got some stories.

CHAPARRO. I love a good story.

LLORENTE. Come on then, I'll give you a song.

BENITO. What is it?

MENDO. I'm just going to close my eyes . . .

LLORENTE (*singing, with* OTHERS *joining*).
  Oh Jesus my nose will lead me that way,
  Oh Jesus my nose will lead me astray!
  The young girl lurks behind locked doors
  Smelling of fresh green grass
  The married one with her smile so bright
  Smells of hay as she walks past.

  CASILDA *comes in from the back of the house and goes
  upstairs.*

  Oh Jesus my nose will lead me that way,
  Oh Jesus my nose will lead me astray!
  The spinster who sleeps all on her own
  Smelling of fish and of soap
  The widow remembers what honey is like

But smells now of dried old oats.
Oh Jesus my nose will lead me that way,
Oh Jesus my nose will lead me astray!

Some quiet guitar music. Silence. Time passes. A whistle.

LUJAN (*to the* SLEEPING MEN). Are you asleep? (*Aside.*)
(They are, I'm sure. Night – do your best for love. And for
me.) Are you there Commander?

COMMANDER. Here.

LUJAN. Come on in.

COMMANDER. I'm in.

LUJAN. You could drive a cart through here they'd not notice.

COMMANDER. I don't know where I am – show me the way.

LUJAN. Leonardo can't come – he needs to stay here.

LEONARDO. Fine. That's fine.

LUJAN. This way.

COMMANDER. To my Fate – wish me luck.

COMMANDER *and* LUJAN *go further into house.*
LEONARDO *hides himself out of the way.*

LLORENTE. Mendo.

MENDO. Yes?

LLORENTE. There's people in the house.

MENDO. I heard them. Pedro will kill us.

LLORENTE. Not our sort either.

MENDO. What d'you mean?

LLORENTE. A gold cape . . .

MENDO. Oh christ – that's the Commander!

LLORENTE. Let's wake the others.

MENDO. No! We can't if it's the Commander.

LLORENTE. No. Are you sure it's him?

MENDO. Who else would dare?

LLORENTE. What should we do?

MENDO. I don't know. It might not be Casilda's fault – if you know what I mean.

LLORENTE. Ssh. They're coming back.

COMMANDER *and* LUJAN *reappear.*

COMMANDER. Damn!

LEONARDO. What happened?

COMMANDER. The witch.

LEONARDO. Why?

COMMANDER. She's locked the door. Sorceress.

LEONARDO. Call her.

COMMANDER. If the house wasn't full of peasants I would!

LEONARDO. You won't wake them – they're labourers. Not the sharpest bunch by daylight. After wine and a day's work there's no chance. What's that? That's a window!

COMMANDER. No, it's all going wrong.

LEONARDO. It might be her –

COMMANDER. Oh God it might –

CASILDA (*from the window*). Who is that? Is it time to get up?

COMMANDER. Not yet. Not yet time. But you appear, the sun does too, so daybreak must be close.

CASILDA. Who are you?

COMMANDER. I'm here for harvest. We're so sorry – not me, all of us – that you're alone tonight. How could he leave you, your husband? He can't really love you. If he did, he couldn't leave you. If the Commander of Ocana had Peribanez' unimaginable luck, 'though you look at him as if he were a Devil, he couldn't walk away from a face like yours, ever. He could never leave you alone, even if the

King ordered him to. Because – because he loves you. The Commander of Ocana worships you.

CASILDA. What are you saying? Don't invite mischief into your life. If you're here to cut wheat, get your scythe by the neck, pick up your gloves and fetch yourself out to the fields. Wheat's your business, and nothing else here between the earth and the stars.

What do you mean the Commander of Ocana loves a peasant? You mock him. How can you say he worships me? Do you think the woman he loves would wear a crocheted apron and worn-down slippers? The Commander would write poems to his lady in black ink italics, not jump her down from a cart at the edge of the vineyard. He'll love an elegant beauty with wavy hair, pinned high with silver combs. Who'd have lace round her neck and be sweet with perfume. Not mint or thyme. Do you think her hands would be rough and flaky, smelling of soap from scrubbing floors? No!

And anyway let me tell you this peasant woman wouldn't want carriages or perfume or gloves. Or poems or combs.

You say he loves me, the Commander, well if he does you tell him if he loved me more than life, virtue or truth, I love Peribanez more in his dirty clothes than I could ever love the Commander with his golden cape. I'd rather know my husband with his filthy collar and matted hair, rabbits hanging from his saddle and the dog barking than the Commander, clean and proud in his feathered hat, offering me his hand.

I've spoken too much. Go now and don't come back. If Pedro heard what you said you wouldn't live to see the sun rise.

The COMMANDER *holds up some jewels in the early morning light for* CASILDA *to see.*

COMMANDER. Look! A necklace – it's pearl. Can you see? And this – gold – they're for you. Let me in. Please! Casilda . . .

CASILDA (*to the* REAPERS, *shouting*). Time to get up! All of you. Up, now! Dawn's here. Are you awake? Come on – let me hear you awake. Whoever cuts the most today, I'll give you Pedro's hat! Come on all of you – Get up!

MENDO. That's Casilda.

LUJAN (*to* COMMANDER). Get going – quickly!

COMMANDER *and* LEONARDO *move away from the house.*

BENITO. Up you get you lazy bull breath.

CHAPARRO. Can a man not meet the dawn in peace?

HELIPE. She's here. Look – mountains – whites of their eyes are already pink.

LLORENTE. Come on slackers. Get up – get up, get up, get up!

COMMANDER (*outside*). I risk my life for her in the middle of the night – my name, my reputation. I'd mix my blood with hers and she tries to expose me! The snake. (*He catches his breath.*) What am I doing?

You won't say no to me again Casilda. You won't do that again.

Scene Four

The PAINTER*'s house in Toledo.*

PAINTER. That's fine. I'll replace the hand and while that's drying I can paint the face and sort the dog and the loaf out – and we'll use the twine on the angel rather than make a new one?

ANTON. Yes – we don't have long in Toledo.

PAINTER. Right, well I'll get straight to work then and see what we can do before the morning.

PERIBANEZ. Before we – of all your pictures there's one that sticks in my mind. Probably because I'm a working man and the picture is of a peasant woman – but the detail . . . I'd like to see it again, would you mind? Before we go.

PAINTER. Ah I'm quite proud of that one. She's also a very beautiful subject of course –

PERIBANEZ. Could you get it down? I'd like Anton to see it –

ANTON. I did. But go ahead, if you want to see it again.

PAINTER. I'll fetch her for you, if she's willing to come . . . !

PERIBANEZ (*to* ANTON). She's like an angel, you watch.

    PAINTER *goes.*

ANTON. I'm not surprised you want to see that one again.

PERIBANEZ. How d'you know my taste in paintings? It's just the dress, it looks –

ANTON. Come on Pedro – It looks like Casilda.

PERIBANEZ. Casilda's not as beautiful as that is she?

ANTON. You're her husband – don't make me praise her for you.

    PAINTER *re-enters with the portrait of* CASILDA.

PAINTER. There she goes.

PERIBANEZ (*aside*). (My undoing.)

PAINTER. Yes, I'm fond of this one I must say.

PERIBANEZ. It's very good. Anton?

ANTON. A fine painting.

    Small silence.

PERIBANEZ (*to* ANTON). You go back to the Inn and feed the horses – I want to stay a bit longer.

ANTON. Right. (*Aside.*) (That's no-one but Casilda. He's burning alive poor man). See you soon then.

    ANTON *exits.*

PERIBANEZ. How did you make such a beautiful picture? The eyes, her mouth. Her hair. Where was she from, this woman?

PAINTER. Well now I'm wondering whether it's such a good likeness after all because actually, she's from the same town as you.

PERIBANEZ. Ocana?

PAINTER. Yes, Ocana.

PERIBANEZ. There is someone there who looks like this but it can't be her because she's recently married and I'm sure her husband couldn't afford a portrait of her.

PAINTER. Well yes that might be her. I don't really know, I didn't meet her, I had to paint her without her knowing – on a small sketch pad first, not, obviously, straight on to canvas – that would have been a bit conspicuous . . . no, I did her in secret and then expanded it into this painting.

PERIBANEZ. I think I know who asked you to paint her. Will you tell me if I'm right?

PAINTER. Um – I shouldn't really . . .

PERIBANEZ. Was it the Commander of Ocana?

PAINTER. Well – she knew nothing about it, I guess there's no harm – yes, it was him. A very impressive man. One of the best soldiers in Spain of course, and completely absorbed in this peasant girl!

PERIBANEZ. But she doesn't know that? She doesn't know about the picture?

PAINTER. Not a whisper. I suppose he can't declare his love to her because she belongs to somebody else. And not ready to stray it seems, otherwise my job would have been a lot easier!

PERIBANEZ. Can I take it back with me?

PAINTER. They haven't paid me yet.

PERIBANEZ. I'll pay – how much is it?

PAINTER. I'm not sure the, um, Commander, would like that much. He's sending his man to collect it some time tomorrow.

PERIBANEZ. His man? Is he, by any chance, a short man with dark brows?

PAINTER. Now that's certainly one of his men. Bushy brows? He's the one who employed me.

PERIBANEZ. I knew I recognized him.

PAINTER. Who, the one with bushy brows?

PERIBANEZ. I saw him, in my own house. He came to my house yesterday –

PAINTER. Did he?

PERIBANEZ. Turned up for harvest. I nearly said something – and now I'm here, hours away, in Toledo.

PAINTER. Well I'd better start back to work – I've a long evening ahead. Is that everything?

PERIBANEZ. While you're fixing the statue I'd like to come and see this picture again. A thousand times.

PAINTER (*laughs a little nervously*). Of course, feel free – whenever you like.

PERIBANEZ. Thank you. Goodbye.

Scene Four and a Half

PERIBANEZ *is alone.*

PERIBANEZ. Backwards, go backwards, time unravel. Please not my mind, oh God. Don Fadrique has a painting of my wife. Just that leaves me sliced open to the vultures. But if she didn't know – does she not know? – maybe nobody knows. Maybe nobody knows. This is the cost of her beauty. Is the price of peace to marry a wife you don't love?

He's robbed me of my peace dear God. Casilda, my Queen. This is so ugly, this jealousy. I don't want it to be seen, I don't want anyone to know what he wants, what he wants to do with her. It's like he's had her already. Chewed her up and spat her out. I have to stop. He should protect me – he's my Lord. I serve him – he offers me honour and I serve him – not splay me open this way, hounded out of my home by laughter and contempt. If I leave Ocana, start a new life far from this nightmare, how will I live without my farm? Can I start again with nothing? I can't creep quietly back to my farm and home amongst whispers and gossip – everything I loved becomes my enemy. I need to talk to Casilda. Is she more than I deserve? What a stupid man I am. How could I think she could have been mine? That she was mine? How stupid to think that powerful wealth wouldn't want her too. Flick his envious eyes over her sweet face. Where would he flick his tongue? This will kill me. If this is what paint does, the real thing will send me to Hell. Christ! Help me Saint Roque. I can't live with this. God protect me I'll kill him. Stupid stupid why was I so stupid?

Interval.

Scene Five

The COMMANDER's *house the following day. The* COMMANDER *has a letter.*

COMMANDER. Two hundred, on his Majesty's instructions.

LEONARDO. We can manage that.

COMMANDER. We'll issue a proclamation. A hundred nobles willing to fight for their Church and Country – and a hundred peasants.

LEONARDO. Peasants?

COMMANDER. You don't get it.

LEONARDO. I guess not.

COMMANDER. Why not peasants? It's their country too. And
if we send a hundred peasants, don't we need a dependable,
trustworthy, brave farmer to lead that peasant troop?

LEONARDO. You'd send a hundred peasants in to battle to get
Peribanez out the way? Love is turning your mind Sir.

COMMANDER. Love sharpens the mind to a cutting edge.
It requires disciplined strategy, like war. Is he back from
Toledo yet?

LEONARDO. I . . . tonight, Lujan tells me. But Sir the King
is expecting you at the palace.

COMMANDER. Find out. I have to catch him before they
have time to talk – he can't know about my visit, we've got
to send him away.

LEONARDO. She won't tell him. Casilda and Ines – they've
agreed not to trouble him with it. Casilda is tearful, jumpy,
restless, worried – all good signs.

COMMANDER. I need to see her!

LEONARDO. You will. It's time for Ines to tell her our
marriage plans – she'll have to meet you for that otherwise
no wedding – she can't refuse her cousin.

COMMANDER. She'll do what she wants, she's made of
granite!

Leonardo I've been useless since waking and seeing her
face.

LEONARDO. Yes. You'll have her. And she'll be sweeter for
the chase. Troy was impenetrable but the horse made rubble
of its walls. Didn't it? Peasants are simple beings with
diminutive souls. They learn to deny themselves what they
most want in the world – they have to, they've no money –
when something comes along that they *can* have it takes
them a while to see. Don't worry. We will, if you're serious,
send Peribanez to war, and she'll open for you like an
oyster.

COMMANDER. I hope you're right. I'm like a child. I'll lead a troop through the hell of battle but this woman – I'm a baby struggling on its back.

Find out if Ines has more news. Babies learn to walk – I will see this through.

LEONARDO. Take heart. Your love will be satisfied.

LEONARDO *exits.*

COMMANDER. Will it? I'm the King who loves a tree. The man whose only friend was a statue. He couldn't leave her side. Night after night telling all his heart's sorrows to stone. They could touch them, wrap their arms, hold them tight. Enviable men. My tree is an ivy, clinging to another. But I can't walk away. I'll die before I do.

Scene Six

PERIBANEZ *and* ANTON *by a field with their horses and the mule with San Roque.*

PERIBANEZ. Get home to your wife – I want to check on the men.

ANTON. I'll come with you.

PERIBANEZ. No. Leave the Saint – I'll take it to the Church then get the animals fed. I'm going to the fields first.

ANTON. You've got your own Saint waiting for you up at the house. I'll drop him off, you get home – you're the newly married one.

PERIBANEZ. You go. Knock on our door and tell Casilda I'm at the fields and I'll be back later. I need to speak to the men.

ANTON. Pedro . . .

A pause.

God be with you.

PEDRO. And you Anton.

ANTON *leaves, taking his horse with him.*

PERIBANEZ. If it's not Casilda's fault why don't I want to see
her? All this because of your loveliness. If you weren't the
girl you are . . .

My ripe fields. When I sowed you I was filled with hope,
full of joy. Building our nest for the winter. The river of my
life was in high unstoppable flow. Now there's this dam in
the middle of the water – it's killing me.

A strain of music far off.

Somebody singing will wring me dry.

The REAPERS *are making their way in from the fields.*

PERIBANEZ. They're coming this way. Of course they are,
it's nearly dark, stupid man.

HELIPE (*singing*).
Pedro's wife, Pedro's wife, Pedro's gorgeous wife.

PERIBANEZ. No, God, no, not that. (*He hides.*)

LLORENTE (*singing*)
Pedro's wife is the beauty of the town,
Commander at her window – she met him with a frown,
Not just beautiful but virtuous as well,
Pedro's wife is a rare and precious pearl.
Pedro's wife, Pedro's wife, Pedro's gorgeous blessed wife.
Commander says he wants her only for himself,
Casilda says 'be gone Sir for the sake of your good health'
Pedro's in Toledo, Commander's out to impress,
Casilda takes one look at him and this is what she says:
'I love my Pedro more Sir, with his hare and pheasant,
Than you in all your finery, covered in sweet scent,
I'd have his woollen cape against my skin on any day
Than all your silks and feathers Sir – now get you on your
    way!'s
Oh Pedro's wife, Pedro's wife, Pedro's gorgeous blessed wife,
Pedro's wife, Pedro's wife, Pedro's gorgeous wife.

The reapers have left the fields, passed PEDRO, *hidden,*
and are on their way home, leaving him on his own again.

PEDRO. That's it – as it would have happened. I'm a lucky
man. Thank you Heaven for my wife. Casilda's an angel
and they know it. But still they're singing about her. Us.
And it shakes my sickened soul.

Scene Seven

PERIBANEZ' *house.*

CASILDA. I can't believe what you're trying to say to me.

INES. How d'you know – you won't let me speak?

CASILDA. I don't want to hear it – what do you expect?

INES. You're so puffed up on Pedro's love, you leap to protect
him when no-one's trying to hurt him – I'm not asking you
to meet the Commander because of you – I'm saying meet
him because of me!

CASILDA. You?

INES. You're not the only woman in the world with love in her
life –

CASILDA. You mean?

INES. Yes. Yes!

CASILDA. Ines I'm going mad. I don't know what I'm thinking,
I'm sorry. But if it's about you then tell me – tell me.

INES. The Commander's gentleman – Leonardo – he loves me.
He wants to marry me.

CASILDA. Oh Ines – how could you fall for that.

INES. He loves me I said. More than life itself.

CASILDA. He's lying to you!

INES. I've got it in writing!

CASILDA. Words and ink Ines are like dust in the wind. Why d'you think he's after you? You're not rich, or noble – and Ocana is stuffed full of women who are.

INES. Thank you cousin. And for your willingness to help. If you're this stinging with the Commander he's never going to marry us!

CASILDA. That is what he wants you to say to me. That's exactly why his 'gentleman' is pretending to be in love with you. They'll say anything – they don't care – they'll sing us to our deaths!

INES. What's dishonourable about speaking nicely to a Commander? I'm not asking you to run out in the moonlight and meet him at the gate, I'm not even saying talk to him at the window.

CASILDA. That's enough.

INES. What have you got to lose? Because Casilda I've got my life's happiness at stake and all you have to do is speak civilly to him . . .

CASILDA. I said enough! You never look at his face or mention his name again and Ines if you do you aren't welcome in my house!

INES *is stung to the core.*

Oh God cousin – if I see him I'll listen to him, and mad stupid words can lead to *doing* stupid things, bad things of regret and shame.

Enter PERIBANEZ.

PERIBANEZ. Wife.

CASILDA. Pedro! Light of my life.

PERIBANEZ. How have you been?

CASILDA. Without you. How was your journey?

PERIBANEZ. A lot better now I'm here. Ines.

INES. Hello Pedro.

PERIBANEZ. What more can a man ask. Two lovely ladies here together awaiting my return.

CASILDA. My lovely cousin has stayed with me ever since you left.

PERIBANEZ. We'll buy ourselves new shoes when she gets married. Dance in silver shoes. That's what people do isn't it?

CASILDA. So what did you bring back?

PERIBANEZ. My hopes. Which were so heavy I couldn't fit all your jewels and dresses onto the horse. But I did squeeze in . . . (*Produces a pair of open-toed shoes.*) these. I hope they fit. Mother of pearl buckles. And . . . (*produces two long sashes and a hair comb*), because I love you.

CASILDA. Oh Pedro, they're beautiful.

PERIBANEZ. I had an accident on the way back. Lucky I'm still alive – a miracle really.

CASILDA. What happened?

PERIBANEZ. The horse stumbled – I slipped off the road.

CASILDA. Oh God. Where?

PERIBANEZ. San Roque must have saved me. He's the reason I went . . .

CASILDA. I'm going cold.

PERIBANEZ. As I scrambled back on to the horse I promised to give up the best thing we had in our house to him. I want to take the hangings off the walls – we don't need them – and put San Roque up instead, in thanks. A painting of him maybe.

CASILDA. Of course, let's take them down. All of them – if they were covered with rubies.

PERIBANEZ. Anyway I don't think it's right to have somebody else's banners on our walls. I don't want everyone gossiping about some peasant farmer and his wife surrounding their bed with the Commander's coats of Arms.

Who are we to have castles and armies on our walls – how many Arabs have we killed? We should have crosses made from wheat at harvest time – not great red embroidered ones – it's wrong. If it's red we're after, put a poppy in a vase. You can't plough a field up with feathers. And we should have icons – painted icons, why not? The annunciation, the assumption. San Francisco, San Blas, San Sebastian, San Roque . . . so many we could choose from. We don't need Arms.

I don't mean portraits – portraits are like ghosts on the wall. I saw one in Toledo – I nearly bought it –

CASILDA. Pedro, are you –

PERIBANEZ. Never mind. Supper. Let's have supper Casilda, then I'm going straight to bed. I'm tired.

INES *looks embarrassed.*

CASILDA (*to* PEDRO). Are you feeling alright love?

PERIBANEZ. Yes, fine. Who's this?

LUJAN *enters in his reaper clothes.*

LUJAN. There's someone at the door to see you from the Commander's house.

PERIBANEZ. From who?

LUJAN. From the Commander of Ocana.

PERIBANEZ. What does he want – at this time of night?

LUJAN. I don't know. I guess if you let him in you'll find out.

PERIBANEZ. Why are you telling me – why not one of the others?

LUJAN. Uh, I was closest to the door Sir.

PERIBANEZ. You're the reaper that came on Monday.

LUJAN. I am. (*Aside.*) (Why's he looking at me like that?)

PERIBANEZ. So the Commander wants me?

LUJAN. No, the man out in the hall does.

PERIBANEZ (*aside*). (Slippery as wet glass, honour.)

(*To* CASILDA.) Eat without me. I'm not hungry anyway.

(*Aside*.) (However close we hold it, however much we care,
It slides to the floor – we're holding thin air.)

PERIBANEZ *exits, with* LUJAN.

ACT THREE

Scene One

A town square in Ocana.

LEONARDO. Sir . . .

COMMANDER. I'm listening. For God's sake keep it brief.

LEONARDO. I'll try.

COMMANDER. I should welcome the distraction from chewing my own brains.

LEONARDO. The King – Enrique the Just they're now calling him – has letters from Granada saying the Arabs aren't moving from Ayamonte. Nor will they pay their tributes. So Enrique wants to take Ayamonte as his starting point for the campaign and carry on from there. He's very serious – he wants to make a campaign befitting Spain's greatest ever King . . . Which is why he summoned the court in Toledo.

COMMANDER. Go on.

LEONARDO. They're still arriving, leaders from all over. I – gave your apologies.

Meanwhile, in the Royal Castle, Enrique was holding a small but potent meeting to discuss the finer details of strategy.

COMMANDER. Who was there?

LEONARDO. Ruy Lopez de Avalos, both the King's cousins – the Duke of Arjona and don Enrique Manuel – who could flatten the Moors between them. The Constable of Castille, no surprise there, and Enrique's confederacy of judges – Pedro Sanchez of Castille, Perianez of Aragon, Rodriguez of –

COMMANDER. Stop. What do you mean Peribanez?

LEONARDO. Sir, I'm talking about the King's judges –
Perianez being one of them – do you think our Ocanan
peasant could judge the King?

COMMANDER. My blood curdled. That's enough, my heart's
not in it. The King's going to march Castille's finest fighters
against the borders of Ayamonte, continuing on from there
getting rid of all the non-tribute paying Arabs from Spain?

LEONARDO. Exactly.

COMMANDER. Good. Well while you were away I executed
my plan. Peribanez is now the proud captain of a hundred
peasants. Which generally thrilled everybody. Why not? It's
a first – peasant farmer turns captain – regardless of its
dubious spawning. He spent the paltry money he has on a
uniform and yesterday, quick off the mark, gathered his men
and had them out in the square parading. I learn from Lujan
that he's marching them to Toledo today.

LEONARDO. Leaving behind him a little something for you.
Pig-headed and ungrateful 'though she is.

COMMANDER. Love's absence, I hope, like a stone in water
will wear the diamond down.

The sound of drums is heard.

LEONARDO. Whose . . . ?

COMMANDER. His. Your lieutenant is bringing the others
soon. Get your arms on Leonardo, so Pedro thinks you're
marching out with them.

LEONARDO. He's here. Back soon.

LEONARDO *exits.* PERIBANEZ *enters with a dagger and
a sword;* BENITO *and* LLORENTE *are with him.*

PERIBANEZ. I've come to take leave of you my Lord.

COMMANDER. That's thoughtful.

PERIBANEZ. I go in your honour Sir.

COMMANDER. You go in service of the King.

PERIBANEZ. His and yours.

COMMANDER. Of course.

PERIBANEZ. The King calls us to war but it's you who's honoured me. How could I dream of being a Captain? My name would never even have reached the ears of the King. He's greater than I can imagine and here I am carrying his flag. May God preserve you.

COMMANDER. And you Pedro, may he bring you success in this campaign.

Small silence.

PERIBANEZ. Do I look alright in these clothes?

COMMANDER. Very good. There's nothing to choose between us.

PERIBANEZ. There's something I want to ask you – I don't know if you'll oblige me –

COMMANDER. Ask and we'll see.

PERIBANEZ. I'd like you to strap on my sword for me. I want to take your protection with me.

COMMANDER. I'll do better than that – I'll make you a knight. I expect you to make a fine soldier Pedro, a spirited man like you.

PEDRO. I . . . It's here Sir. If you could just put it on for me.

COMMANDER. Of course – wear it for me.

BENITO. Get down.

LLORENTE. Is something wrong?

BENITO. You – get down quick.

COMMANDER (*he has buckled* PERIBANEZ' *sword on for him*). There we are.

PERIBANEZ. Thank you Commander.

LLORENTE. Does this make Pedro a gentleman?

BENITO. God knows – out of my experience. It's not something mules do to each other.

COMMANDER (*he takes* PERIBANEZ' *sword from its holder and proceeds to knight him with it*). Do you swear to use this sword in service of God our supreme Lord, and the King?

PERIBANEZ. I swear this and more. I swear to wear this sword in defence of my honour – the honour which you are bound to protect as Lord of this land. I'm leaving my house and my wife in your care while I'm away. I entrust them to you because they mean more to me than my life and, why would anyone harm them? But Sir I'm pleased to know that you'll guard them for me.

You understand honour. Self-respect. You know it's worth everything – beyond riches or happiness.

I'm away fighting at your command but you've put my sword on for me. I take that to mean I have your permission to use my sword to protect my honour.

COMMANDER. Freely. You have my permission freely. I'm sure you'll use it wisely.

PEDRO. So onwards to war, and to whatever else may come.

PERIBANEZ *exits with* BENITO *and* LLORENTE.
COMMANDER *is left alone.*

COMMANDER. Get out jaundiced guilt – of course he wasn't threatening me! What can he do? He's a peasant. He should be proud I want his wife! Casilda you're mine tonight. Your 'best man in the world' is going and nothing's to stop me. I'll kill the man who tries.

COMMANDER *exits.* CASILDA, COSTANZA *and* INES *appear in the square, on a balcony.*

COSTANZA. I can't believe he's going.

CASILDA. Well he is. Leaving me to fight a war on my own. He should stay and beat his drums at home.

INES. Oh come on – he's a Captain Casilda!

CASILDA. Yes. I wish he wasn't.

COSTANZA. I've never heard of anyone like us being given all those titles and jobs and stuff. Doesn't he only have to march as far as Toledo?

CASILDA. D'you think I'd survive if it was further?

INES. Is that his drum?

COSTANZA. Anyway, it's the poor men marching with him you should feel sorry for, not yourself.

Enter PERIBANEZ *with his drums, a flag and* LLORENTE *and* BENITO.

BENITO. Look at those young chickens. It brings air to my lungs just seeing them. Not that they'd be interested nowadays. Not sure I'd be up for it either.

PERIBANEZ. Peaked have you Benito?

BENITO. Lost the taste.

PERIBANEZ. Temporary I'm sure. Your old cape doesn't fool me.

BENITO. Well Captain, I'm grateful for your high estimation. Time was . . . summers past . . .

CASILDA (*to* PEDRO). There's my gallant captain.

PERIBANEZ (*to* CASILDA). There's the lady for whom I carry this sword.

CASILDA. You're leaving us senor.

PERIBANEZ. Senora I am. Taking my heart, my soldiers, and my watchful mind.

CASILDA. Those three should keep you safe. I wish I could ease the frown from your brow.

PERIBANEZ. My frown? There's always room for doubt in a man's mind. I think you know why. Do you?

CASILDA. Do I?

PERIBANEZ. It's not you – if my dark thoughts doubted you they wouldn't be going anywhere, or me with them. But

I am going and they're coming with me. So. I have to say goodbye to you, and to tell you – I leave you in your own strong hands - where better? I'll always be with you.

Do you think I've changed? Is it odd to have a husband who's a captain – a knight even! – when last week I was up to my knees in grape juice? Did you think you'd ever see this in my hand (*his sword*) or this (*his banner*)? Where every day it's been a stubby sickle with jagged teeth? And here I am, feathers and a plume and this (*his sword*) deadly thing. I'm a nobleman Casilda and... I'm a nobleman now, I know what that means. Do you know who put my sword on for me? The Commander did. Which means he's responsible for protecting all that is mine while I'm gone. And if he does anything less than protect it, then it'll be too much, enough and too much.

CASILDA. Hush Pedro, your words are tumbling out, I can't keep up with you.

INES *is watching* CASILDA. *The sound of an approaching trumpet interrupts* CASILDA.

PERIBANEZ. I want a favour from you. I'm a newly knighted-captain, and you're my lady which means –

CASILDA. A favour. So what can I give you? A peasant girl like me and you a smart Captain?

PERIBANEZ. Don't . . .

CASILDA. Take this ribbon.

PERIBANEZ. A black one Casilda?

CASILDA. Why – is that a bad omen in war?

PERIBANEZ. The worst. Mourning, exile . . .

LLORENTE. What about me? Don't I get a favour Senora Costanza?

COSTANZA. Well . . .

BENITO. Come on then Ines – one for an old soldier –

INES. You'd better bring me back a Moor in return – on a dog-lead.

Sound of the nobles' drums, led by LEONARDO.

INES. Oh, here we go.

COSTANZA. They've got the clothes, but you boys have got the spirit.

PERIBANEZ. Right men, rise to it!

BENITO. We won't let them piss on our straw!

LLORENTE. You should've seen them with the mad bull – show them an Arab and they'll run screaming!

BENITO. Let's take them for a stroll Pedro . . .

PERIBANEZ. Behave boys, know your place. The lance always follows the crossbow.

> PERIBANEZ, LLORENTE *and* BENITO *put themselves in order and start the drum roll, preparing to go and join the company of nobles.*

COSTANZA. Bye Llorente.

> LLORENTE *smiles up at* COSTANZA.

CASILDA. C is for come back soon.

> PERIBANEZ *looks at* CASILDA *and leaves with his men. The girls exit.* LEONARDO *enters, looking for* INES. INES *enters.*

INES. Hello Captain.

LEONARDO. Why have your cousins disappeared?

INES. Take a guess. Not in a good mood. She must be made of rock. Sterner stuff than me anyhow.

LEONARDO. Surely now Pedro's gone – won't she let the Commander come and see her just for a bit?

> INES *looks uncertain.*

Then he'll never marry us!

> LEONARDO *starts to leave, appearing to be upset.*

INES. Wait! Tell the Commander I'll let him in one night when she thinks it could be Pedro home on leave.

LEONARDO. The Commander's dying back there! He's half the man he was. How long can he take sick leave when he's in perfect health?

INES. Alright! Tell him to come to the street door tonight.

LEONARDO. Fantastic. What's the signal?

INES. A song. A proper one.

LEONARDO. See you later.

INES. Are you coming too?

LEONARDO. Maybe. What's a Lieutenant for?

INES. See you later.

INES *goes in*.

LEONARDO. So. The pig is fattened and off to slaughter.

Scene Two

The COMMANDER*'s house.*

COMMANDER. You saw him leave?

LUJAN. I did. On a very good horse – the fastest of the lot. He was an impressive sight actually, commanding his troops.

COMMANDER. I know, the company's good.

LUJAN. You can venture for her now Sir.

COMMANDER. They'll be in Toledo by tomorrow lunchtime.

LUJAN. If they camped tonight they would be.

COMMANDER. They'll probably keep going. They will won't they? A bunch of peasants, first-time soldiers.

LUJAN. They're used to a long day's work. With the drums going they could get to Granada in one go.

COMMANDER. Then tonight's the night. We've done it. How do I live 'til then?

LUJAN. It's nearly nine already. Don't be unhappy Sir. You'll seize your day – as soon as it's night. All the waiting will melt away. Enjoy these moments – you'll never have this time again, this delicious anticipation . . .

COMMANDER. It's Hell when you wait this long.

LUJAN. Sorry Sir.

Is Leonardo coming tonight?

COMMANDER. Do you not understand anything thick-head? It's his fiancée – if Ines doesn't open the door, how d'you think we'll get in?

LUJAN. Right. What's the signal?

COMMANDER. Singing. We've got some singers.

LUJAN. Won't that – alert your prey?

COMMANDER. The opposite. The noise will create a diversion so no-one will hear the door.

LUJAN. Can I . . . do you mind if I tell you a story that keeps coming in to my mind?

COMMANDER. What story?

LUJAN. These two families who planned this big wedding – they spent all their money on it, they got the Priest, the player turned up with his best instruments, the groom was excited, the bride's mother and father –

COMMANDER. I get the picture.

LUJAN. But the bride hadn't said yes. She said she was there against her will and when the Priest put the question to her, she answered 'no'. So he asked her again, and again she said 'no'. And d'you know what?

COMMANDER. What?

LUJAN. He asked her a third time and do you know what she said?

COMMANDER. No.

LUJAN. Exactly. So they packed up and went home.

COMMANDER. Your point being . . .

LUJAN. I think Casilda needs to say yes. She can be stern –
you've seen it yourself. It's very well organised with
musicians and everything but if she doesn't give –

COMMANDER. The plan is perfectly appropriate. I've asked,
she's refused. If Casilda won't give me her consent, we
have to go about it another way. What else can I do? If you
don't like it go work elsewhere.

LUJAN. No, it's fine, it's just we're walking blind.

FLOREZ *enters with two* MUSICIANS.

FLOREZ. Sir, the singers are here.

LISARDO. Lisardo (*Introduces himself.*) and Valerio,
(*Introduces his friend.*) yours until day break.

COMMANDER. Ah friends, here to take part in my plan.
(*Pointing at* LUJAN.) He doesn't like it. All I can say is it
comes from an honourable source (*He places his hand on
his heart.*) and, well it's mine.

VALERIO. We're happy to serve you Sir, and your plan.

COMMANDER. Was that eleven? Did it just strike eleven?

LUJAN. I don't think so . . .

VALERIO. I counted as far as eight.

LUJAN. I just caught the first three.

COMMANDER (*to* LUJAN). You begrudge me every growing
minute, don't you? At least the clock strikes without blame.

LUJAN. We can't change the time Sir.

COMMANDER. I know, of course I know.

LUJAN. Why not have a little supper?

COMMANDER. God curse your Christmases – how can I *eat*?

LUJAN. A drink?

COMMANDER. Is there ice?

FLOREZ. No – no ice . . .

COMMANDER. Go drown on it.

FLOREZ. I've brought your cloak Sir.

COMMANDER. Good. Give me it. What's this?

FLOREZ. Your dark cloak Sir.

COMMANDER. Am I in mourning? What are you trying to say? Everything I look at upsets me!

FLOREZ. Shall I get you another one Sir? A brightly coloured one?

LUJAN. Can I – it's just that – Sir, the discreet lover in these matters of the heart doesn't cover himself in colours – it's the kind of thing that could repeat on you – in court for instance.

COMMANDER. Get me the coloured one monkey! Are you servants or grandmothers?

FLOREZ. It's here Sir, your coloured cloak.

COMMANDER. I am unashamedly Love's servant and willingly I take one night for all the days I've given her.

LUJAN. Do you need me to come with you Sir?

COMMANDER. Yes! Please. Leonardo's disappeared, let's go without him. It'll be dark soon. Your pedantic nature might temper these flames which are currently burning me from the inside out.

Scene Three

Night – a street in Ocana.

PERIBANEZ (*to his* HORSE). My saving grace. The value of
a good horse to a man in Hell – what a friend. I bless the
barley I feed you night and day. Thank you for carrying me
home. Dear horse, you've carried me a thousand times
before but honour kept me light, like a feather. Dignified.
Ignorant. Not anymore. The heaviness on your back now,
me and the weight of my fury – bless you. My men huddled
in tents in Toledo's fields and me back in Ocana, can you
believe it? Can you? Can you, Ocana, swear I have my
honour tonight? What is honour? A gnarled dried stick –
snap – where's the sap gone? Something for deaf people or
neighbours with no tongues. But you, horse, up that hill in
under an hour – you're like the wind! I'll commission a
portrait of you – 'horse with wings'. I'm still heady with the
hours we've travelled, I could cry out – ! No. D'you think
my walls are billowing into Anton's next door, bending
with the weight of my shame? We're here. Hide yourself.
(*He takes the* HORSE *and ties him up out of the way.*)

(*At* ANTON'*s front door.*) Anton – are you there?

ANTON (*to his* WIFE). Did you hear someone?

PERIBANEZ. It's me.

ANTON. Who is it?

PERIBANEZ. It's me, Perib –

ANTON (*to his* WIFE). Whatever it is I've got to open the
door.

PERIBANEZ. Ssh, don't panic, it's me.

ANTON. Who is it?

PERIBANEZ. Perib – I can't spit my name out for shame.

ANTON (*opens door*). You're lucky I'm not stark naked. I'm
up so early tomorrow I went to bed in my clothes. How can
I help you my friend?

PERIBANEZ. I need to get into my house through yours. You know why.

ANTON. I do. I didn't say much, I know. But Pedro, Casilda is –

PERIBANEZ. An angel!

ANTON. Then look after her.

PERIBANEZ. Brother, don't start –

ANTON. Come in. I open this door because I know her.

PERIBANEZ. You know what I know. I am hers, for always.

ANTON. Where are your soldiers?

PERIBANEZ. In Toledo with the Lieutenant. I came back alone – with my demons. How did the horse get us all here, there's so many. Enough for madness to feast off God help me.

They go in to ANTON*'s house. The* COMMANDER, LUJAN *carrying a shield and the* MUSICIANS *appear.*

COMMANDER. Start now. The wind will carry it.

The MUSICIANS *begin softly.*

Jesus I can feel my blood easing in my veins.

LISARDO *and* VALERIO (*singing*).
    Floored by a bull and brought to your door
    Sweet bride, sweet bride,
    Your wedding feast served me up
    And brought me to your side.
    The whole town gasped and watched me fall
    But you the loveliest of them all
    Irreverent and grave you were
    With no 'God Bless you Sir'
    No, no 'God Bless you Sir.'

INES appears at the window. The music continues.

INES. That's enough!

COMMANDER. Is that Ines?

INES. Yes it is.

COMMANDER. My soul's in torment Ines and I'm a man, not a ghost, so whatever you need to do, whatever prayers you need to utter, spit them out quickly and deliver me from Hell.

INES. You're early. Where's Leonardo?

COMMANDER. Not here yet. Watching for the husband. Open up Ines, let me see her and you'll get your Leonardo.

INES. Will he be long?

COMMANDER. No. I said, he's looking out for Peribanez.

INES. Pedro wiii be in Toiedo won't he? Parading in his captain's uniform . . .

COMMANDER. She's probably sleeping is she? Can I – put me out my misery – let me in.

INES. Go on then, in you come. I wanted to see if Leonardo was coming first.

LUJAN. What about me?

INES. Come on, the pair of you.

COMMANDER (*to* MUSICIANS). You can stop now Lisardo. See you tomorrow.

COMMANDER *and* LUJAN *go inside with* INES.

LISARDO. Good luck. May you have your small piece of Heaven.

VALERIO. Where to now?

LISARDO. Bed.

VALERIO. She was lovely!

LISARDO. We've got to keep this quiet.

VALERIO. I'm wide awake now. Lucky dog!

Scene Four

In the shadows of PERIBANEZ' *back-yard.*

PERIBANEZ. It's quiet in there. Are you sleeping – wife? I've broken in, creeping round like a thief in our house. The geese are awake, it's getting noisy outside. The animals – they know, they feel me sinking – I'm their master. The pig's snorting, the cows are rumbling – it'll get worse. The laws of nature are disturbed you see. You're my wife, not the Commander's. You're not his, however rich, however thick his blood. (*He listens.*) Your blood. Are you there? Commander Sir?

He moves further in to the house. ·

Even the donkey's tugging his rope. I'm a man who breaks into his own house. I thought the cockerel would wake up – that you'd hear him. I was ready to kill if he went off. But I found him in the half dark and he was asleep, with thirty hens around him. A whole sea of hens! I can't sleep for fear of losing one and there he is, sleeping in bliss, surrounded by his fortune ready for anyone to take. I hated him. His ease and his red crest. The same, the same red cross on your magnificent chest that took four women a full week to sew.

He listens again.

Is she asleep or am I too late? I want to cry.

He hears voices and climbs into a big sack of flour to hide.

CASILDA. I know I heard someone.

INES. And I know you didn't.

CASILDA. You were talking to a man.

INES. I was?

CASILDA. Yes, I heard you!

INES. Me and a man?

CASILDA. If I'm wrong then it's thieves.

INES. Don't Casilda, you're scaring me.

CASILDA. Scream.

INES. I'm not screaming.

CASILDA. Then I will.

INES. And wake Anton and everyone up for no reason?

Enter the COMMANDER *and* LUJAN.

COMMANDER. I can't stay away any more – I have to have
you. I'm the Commander, Casilda, I'm your master –

CASILDA. What are you doing here? I've got one master on
earth and that's Pedro.

COMMANDER. I don't care – I'm here as your slave. Take
me in Casilda or I'll say I caught you with this servant.

CASILDA. You don't scare me, with your thunder and
lightning. (*To* INES.) What have you done you stupid girl?

INES (*very scared*). Come on Casilda – you can't blame me.
He's here now. You're a peasant, your husband's a farmer
and here's a Prince dying for want of you! He's here in your
house and you can save him. His life's more precious than
your honour Casilda. Pedro's in Toledo.

CASILDA. What are you, mistress of a whore-house? My own
cousin's a scorpion.

COMMANDER. Let me alone with her.

INES. No, that's not what –

COMMANDER (*to* LUJAN). Take her out.

LUJAN (*to* INES). Let's leave them. They can sort it out on
their own together.

INES. No, I want to stay –

LUJAN *forces* INES *out of the room.*

CASILDA. Remember I'm a Captain's wife – don't come any
closer – I said don't – I'll bite, I'll kick, I'll make you –

The COMMANDER *grabs hold of* CASILDA *and roughly gets most of her clothes off and some of his own so he can put himself in her.*

COMMANDER. I want you so much Casilda –

CASILDA. No! No! No, no, leave me, no –

COMMANDER. Quiet now. Casilda I need you, don't shout!

Enter PERIBANEZ, *still in his captain's uniform and covered in flour.*

PERIBANEZ *(aside)*. (What else do I need? Why am I waiting? I'm a farmer, who works like a dog, that's all I am. Maybe I should talk to him. Or maybe I should just kill him.)

Commander forgive me.

COMMANDER *looks up at* PERIBANEZ; PERIBANEZ *unsheathes his sword and uses it on the* COMMANDER, *cutting deeply into his chest.*

COMMANDER. Jesus, that's me. Mercy.

PERIBANEZ *(to* CASILDA, *trying to put some of her clothes back on)*. It's alright my love. Here. Come away. Follow me.

CASILDA *looks at* PERIBANEZ, *opens her mouth to speak but closes it again. Nothing comes out.*

PERIBANEZ. Follow me through here.

LUJAN *appears, trying to get to the* COMMANDER. PERIBANEZ *takes up his sword again and pursues* LUJAN *off. The* COMMANDER *sits down, unaware that* CASILDA's *still in the room.*

COMMANDER. There we are. Lord, may your holy blood take pity on me now, I am your servant. Ah. And Lord, I am prompted by this river *(his blood)* to ask forgiveness of a servant of mine.

CASILDA *takes a step towards the* COMMANDER.

CASILDA *(barely audible)*. I – . God be with you.

COMMANDER. Whose is that voice, I wonder.

Enter LEONARDO, *treading flour through the dark house.*
CASILDA *hides.*

LEONARDO. This is chaos. Ines – where are you? Ines? It's
me!

COMMANDER. Leonardo, can you not see me?

LEONARDO. My lord?

COMMANDER. Leonardo.

LEONARDO. What happened to you? You're white as a sheet –
you look as though you're about to pass out.

COMMANDER. I'm not. I'm about to die. No more than a
thief deserves.

LEONARDO (*seeing his wound*). Dear God no – who? Who
cut you?

COMMANDER. I tried to steal an Angel Leonardo – she
wasn't mine.

LEONARDO. Why did you leave without me? Was it him?
The husband? I should've been here. What was he doing in
Ocana? (LEONARDO *tries to bind the wound.*)

COMMANDER. I don't want shouting and revenge. There's
not much left of me. I'm just sitting quietly hoping there
really is an afterlife.

LEONARDO. No Sir . . .

COMMANDER. Don't go hunting him down, don't do
anything, he had reason to kill me –

LEONARDO. I'll kill him!

COMMANDER. Just take me to confession and forget the
vengeance Leonardo. I forgive Peribanez.

LEONARDO. A peasant kills you and I'm not allowed to
touch him? That . . . chokes me.

COMMANDER. I can testify for him – he's no peasant, he's a
gentleman. A knight. I strapped on his sword myself and, he
hasn't misused it.

LEONARDO. Let me take you to the nuns. We'll get help.

COMMANDER. I think it's only God can help me now.

LEONARDO *carries* COMMANDER *off.* CASILDA *is alone in the room and listens to* LUJAN *and* INES *fighting for their lives.*

PERIBANEZ. Don't make this difficult. Both of you have to die as well.

INES. I'm dead already. Pedro, please don't kill me . . .

LUJAN (*entering with flour on him*). Oh unfortunate man Lujan. Now where can you hide?

PERIBANEZ (*entering*). There's no point in running. You're dying tonight whatever you do.

LUJAN. Sir, Captain – why?

PERIBANEZ. Because you lied to me and came here as a reaper.

LUJAN. Oh God forgive me.

PERIBANEZ *kills* LUJAN *brutally and messily. He immediately goes off and drags* INES *back in.*

INES. It's me Pedro . . . Pedro – why me?

PERIBANEZ. Because you betrayed me!

INES (*to* PERIBANEZ). Why are you crying? (PERIBANEZ *moves behind her so he can't see her face.*) Casilda! Oh God, cousin, help me. Casilda! (*He cuts her throat.*)

PERIBANEZ. That's it. That's it. It's done.

Silence.

I have to leave. Will you go with me Casilda?

I'll wrap you up warmly, put you on the back of the horse and, before you know it you'll wake up in Toledo.

My darling. We need to get away from this. It'll look different from far away. I need to change these clothes.

CASILDA *stares down at* INES' *body.* PERIBANEZ *takes his bloody captain's clothes off and returns to his working clothes. He dresses quickly. When he's dressed he leads* CASILDA *out.*

Time passes. Out of the silence comes LEONARDO's *voice.*

LEONARDO. Peribanez? Where are you? Where are you, butcher?

He enters with his sword drawn and sees the dead bodies of INES *and* LUJAN.

LEONARDO. Oh Christ . . .

Scene Five

An inner chamber of Toledo Palace. Early morning.

KING. I think now's the time. If you're ready and our army's prepared, I'd like to sound the alarm today.

CONSTABLE. We're ready your honour.

KING. I'm glad. Then, my friend, let's ring the bells. Wake the troops and gather them. Let's send a shudder along the Tagus. I hope news of their tents – a new Toledo out on the plains – reaches the Arabs and petrifies them. God grant us glory.

CONSTABLE. I know that our detachments will be pleased Sir – they're keen to get going. I'll do that straightaway then Sir. (*He makes to leave.*)

The QUEEN *enters.*

QUEEN. Are you busy?

The CONSTABLE *bows to her and exits.*

KING. I – you're always welcome. How is he this morning?

QUEEN. Crying. Tiring. Missing his father.

KING. I'm sorry. He's the future we're fighting for. And the past. I wish he could fight with us –

QUEEN. He's two.

KING. I know. God bless him.

QUEEN. He's your son . . .

KING. Full of your virtues.

QUEEN. I'm hoping he'll adopt most of yours.

KING. We're at war.

QUEEN. Is it today?

CONSTABLE *re-enters*.

KING (*to* CONSTABLE). Whose is that drum?

CONSTABLE. La Ver and Estremadura – just arriving. And fresh arrivals from Guadalajara and Atienza.

KING. Good. And Ocana?

CONSTABLE. There's a problem with Ocana. Half the troops are here – a company of working men, but without their captain. The others are delayed.

KING. Why what's happened?

CONSTABLE. Sir, I've just been told that don Fadrique has been murdered by a peasant.

KING. Don Fadrique?

QUEEN. Are you certain?

CONSTABLE. I wish I could say not, but yes. Certain.

KING. Why on earth? He's our best . . . This is appalling news. A peasant? From his district?

CONSTABLE. Yes. The peasant was jealous of him, apparently.

KING. Jealous? For what reason?

CONSTABLE. I'm sure no reason . . .

QUEEN. Reason and jealousy rarely combine.

KING. Has he been arrested – the peasant?

CONSTABLE. Unfortunately he fled immediately – taking his wife with him.

KING. I come to Toledo – this is not the news one would expect! Is this how Spain responds to my rule?

Put out an order across the city, and in Madrid, Segovia, Talavera and Ocana, that whoever catches the murderer, and his wife, or kills them outright shall be rewarded a thousand new coins. No one must offer them food or shelter or help of any sort, on pain of death.

CONSTABLE. I'll do that right away Sir.

CONSTABLE *exits*.

QUEEN. Oh Enrique . . . (*She moves towards him.*)

KING. How can God protect these people? They must suffer for their crime.

QUEEN. They will – your reward will see that they do.

ARCEO, *the* KING*'s secretary, enters.*

ARCEO. Your standard is ready Sir.

KING. The war begins. Bring it in.

ARCEO *exits and returns with a* PAGE *carrying a red standard which bears the arms of Castille, with a hand carrying a sword above the Arms, and on the other side Christ on the cross.*

ARCEO. Your standard your Majesty.

KING. Thank you. A fine piece of work.

ARCEO *bows and exits.*

As was this Captain. The very best.

QUEEN (*Reading the standard*), 'Enrique the Just'.

Enter CONSTABLE.

CONSTABLE. The orders have gone Sir. Everybody's shocked at the news.

QUEEN. It's enough to make stones cry.

KING. Did he murder him with his scythe? It's unbelievable!

QUEEN. He'll be found Enrique, he can't hide for ever.

KING. And when he *is* I swear his punishment will sear through Spain.

ARCEO *re-enters.*

ARCEO. Your Highness, there's a rural man arrived who says he needs to speak to you.

KING. Right. Bring him in. (*To the* QUEEN.) Good – news already.

PERIBANEZ *enters in his farming clothes, with* CASILDA, *accompanied by* ARCEO *and two* GUARDS.

CONSTABLE. We'll get him Sir.

PERIBANEZ. Great Sire lend me your feet.

KING. Come up – what's your news.

PERIBANEZ. Seeing you Lord I don't know if I can say what I've come to say. I am Peribanez.

KING. Yes . . . ?

PERIBANEZ. Pedro Ibanez, from Ocana.

KING (*realising who he is*). Kill this man! Guards – kill him!

QUEEN. No you don't – guards – guards! Not yet.

KING. Hold him. (*To* PERIBANEZ.) You don't have long. You will feel every tortured step of your death.

PERIBANEZ. I understand I have to die but before I do I hoped you would hear me.

QUEEN (*to her husband*). Let him speak.

KING. Every indefensible case deserves a hearing. Go on.

PERIBANEZ. I am a man, Sir, a farmer, a peasant, a husband and, at one time, a happy man. My mother, my father, their parents and theirs before that were of pure Spanish blood, never mixed with anything except the earth. My hands are working, farming hands, my friends are working, farming

friends. My town – has a place for me. I've worked hard
and it's been proud of me, it's come to me with problems,
questions, trusted me with jobs. More than all this my wife
chose me. We were married in May this year. I became her
shepherd before God. She, my wife, is of pure Spanish
blood too, pure Ocanan blood. She has a heart so clear and
a head so wise that people try to resent her, try to be jealous
of her – they can't be – she warms them. And she's
beautiful.

Don Fadrique, the Commander of Ocana, would not have
crossed our doorway but he was thrown off his horse on our
wedding day, chasing one of the wedding bulls, so he came
to our house. I went looking for the priest and Casilda
stayed with him – he was unconscious. When he woke up
Casilda was there and, he wanted her to be his. I didn't
know that then. It seems he wanted my wife with all his
heart. Time went by and he recovered from his fall and
I called on him and he gave me eight banners with his arms
on to thank us. We hung them up on our bedroom walls.
He also gave me two of the best mules I've ever seen. Not
strong enough to pull my sinking honour from the dirt
'though. And for these mules he expected . . . I had to come
to Toledo for two days. The Commander came to my house
the first night I was away and tried to win Casilda. He
brought gifts with him – necklaces. She said to him go
away and never come back. She did nothing wrong. Then
don Fadrique called me in to see him. I'm a peasant but he
told me he'd had letters from you asking for men in this
campaign and he was placing me in charge of a hundred
other peasant men and I was to lead them to Toledo to fight
in your war. This is an honour I never dreamt of, but I knew
why he asked me. He wanted Casilda. I needed to be sure.
I craved certainty. I marched my men here yesterday and
without breathing I turned and rode back to Ocana. I got
home in the dark and, the thing I needed to see was there
and, our house is soiled and diseased and, well now it's a
place of murder too.

She was half naked, her clothes were on the floor, she
was screaming. He was having what wasn't his. I got my

sword which he strapped on for me yesterday morning
and I pushed it deep into his chest. Then there were the
other two.

I took off my Captain's clothes and we rode back here.

I once heard a nobleman say you should always keep two
horses at home in case of eventualities. I didn't know what
he meant but I do now. Who'd be a nobleman and have two
horses and carry a sword to kill people with?

My wife is innocent and deserves to live. This reward . . .
Sir, my wife Casilda has brought me here and she's going
to be widowed by me very shortly – please give the money
to her.

The QUEEN *wipes her face dry. The* KING *looks at the*
QUEEN.

QUEEN. Well, he loves her.

KING (*to* PERIBANEZ). Your honour's very important to you.
It's unusual in a peasant. (*To the* QUEEN.) I agree, it's a
moving tale, and doesn't after all appear to be a crime
which warrants death.

(*To* PERIBANEZ.) We need men like you in the campaign.
I've a mind to have you don your Captain's uniform again
and carry on at the helm of those hundred men. You can
lead them, as you were doing, to Andalucia. Pedro Ibanez of
Ocana I give you your life.

(*Raises* PERIBANEZ *from the ground.*) I grant Peribanez
the gift of his life, and from this day he has the right to use
his sword as he sees fit, both to attack and defend his rights.

PERIBANEZ *is wrong-footed, perturbed.*

(*To* ARCEO.) Give his wife the reward – I keep my pledge.

The KING *looks at* CASILDA. *She doesn't respond.*
ARCEO *bows and leaves.*

A pause. CASILDA *tries to speak but nothing comes out.*

QUEEN. Casilda. It is Casilda? (CASILDA *doesn't speak.*)
I expect you'll be staying in Toledo for a while. Now that

you're a soldier's wife you'll get used to being away from home. Allow me to offer you some of my dresses. Four, should be enough. (*No response from* CASILDA.)

The QUEEN *looks at the* KING.

KING (*to* CASILDA). Your husband's life is spared, Casilda.

CASILDA *looks at* PERIBANEZ, *and says nothing.*

Scene Five and a Half

A room in the palace. Hanging up there is a rich and beautiful dress, and a captain's uniform with boots. PERIBANEZ *watches* CASILDA. *Slowly she begins to undress in front of him, taking off her peasant dress. For a moment it looks like she will move towards* PERIBANEZ, *but she doesn't. She takes her new dress down and looks at it.* PERIBANEZ *is filled with grief as he dresses in his captain's uniform.*

The End.

A Nick Hern Book

This translation of *Peribanez* first published in Great Britain
in 2003 as an original paperback by Nick Hern Books Limited,
14 Larden Road, London W3 7ST, in association with
the Young Vic theatre, London

Front cover photo: *Vicalvaro* (Madrid, 1985) by Ramon Zabalza
from the book *Gypsies Portrayed* published by Photovision

Typeset by Country Setting, Kingsdown, Kent CT14 8ES
Printed and bound in Great Britain by Bookmarque,
Croydon, Surrey

A CIP catalogue record for this book is available from
the British Library

ISBN 1 85459 758 2